CONTROVERSIES IN TEACHING

By the same author:
Open-mindedness and Education

Controversies in Teaching

William Hare
Dalhousie University

WHEATSHEAF BOOKS
Brighton, Sussex, England

THE ALTHOUSE PRESS
London, Ontario, Canada

First published in Great Britain in 1985 by
WHEATSHEAF BOOKS LTD
A MEMBER OF THE HARVESTER PRESS GROUP
Publisher: John Spiers
Director of Publications: Edward Elgar
16 Ship Street, Brighton, Sussex

and in Canada by
THE ALTHOUSE PRESS
Faculty of Education, The University of Western Ontario,
London, Ontario, Canada N6G 1G7

© The Althouse Press, 1985
Editor: P. O'Leary
Editorial Assistant: B. Nelson
Cover Design: Bothwell Graphics

British Library Cataloguing in Publication Data
Hare, William
   Controversies in teaching.
   1. Education—Philosophy—1965-
   I. Title
   370'.1   LB1025.2

ISBN 0-7450-0100-9
ISBN 0-7450-0101-7 Pbk

Canadian Cataloguing in Publication Data
Hare, William.
   Controversies in teaching

Includes bibliographical references.
ISBN 0-920354-11-4

1. Education — Philosophy — 1965- — Addresses, essays, lectures. 2. Teaching — Addresses, essays, lectures. I. Title.

LB1025.2.H37 1984   371'.001   C84-099642-X

All rights reserved

Printed and bound in Canada by The Aylmer Express Ltd.,
17-23 King St., Aylmer, Ontario N5H 1Z9

To the memory of my mother

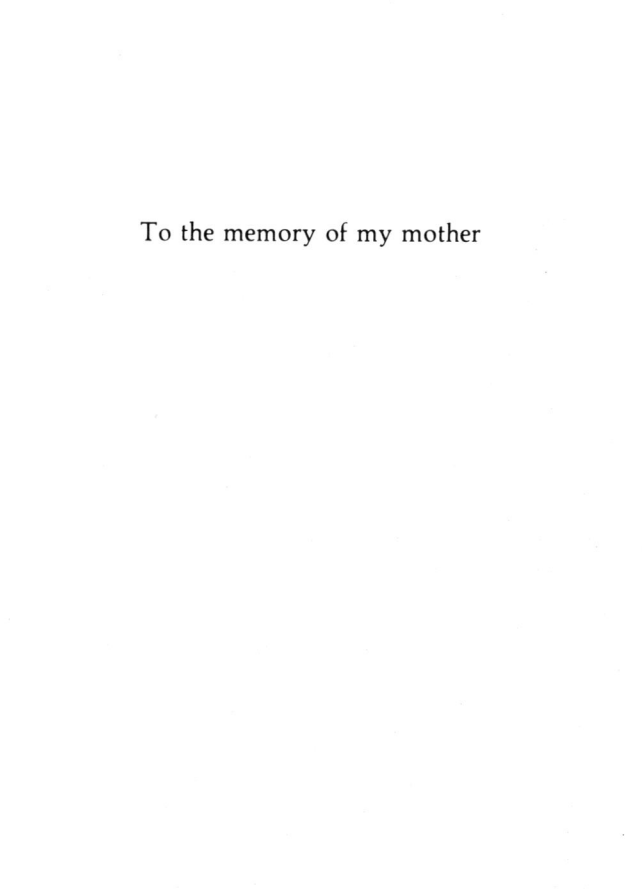

Acknowledgements

1. "Learning: Experience and Enjoyment," from the *Educational Forum*, XXXVII, 3, March 1973, pp. 319-22.
2. "The Criterion of Relevance," from the *Saskatchewan Journal of Educational Research and Development*, 6, 2, Spring 1976, pp. 39-43.
3. "The Concept of Innovation in Education," from *Educational Theory*, 28, 1, Winter 1978, pp. 68-74.
4. "Calling a Halt," from *Educational Studies*, 7, 1, 1976, pp. 62-72.
5. "Appreciation as a Goal of Aesthetic Education," from the *Journal of Aesthetic Education*, 8, 2, April 1974, pp. 5-12.
6. "Education amid Cultural Diversity," from *International Education*, 2, 1, 1972, pp. 36-44.
7. "Education and Cultural Disadvantage," from *Educational Philosophy and Theory*, 11, 1, 1979, pp. 17-21. With the permission of the editors.
8. "Teaching: Preparation and Certification," from *American Secondary Education*, Bowling Green State University, Bowling Green, Ohio, 6, 3, 1976, pp. 38-43. Reprinted by permission.
9. "Models of Field Experience," from *The Teacher Educator*, 10, 1, Autumn 1974, pp. 14-21.
10. "Philosophy as a Vocational Handicap," from *Journal of Education* (Nova Scotia), 3, 2, 1975-6, pp. 22-24.
11. "Controversial Issues and the Teacher," from *The High School Journal*, 57, 2, November 1973. Copyright 1973 The University of North Carolina Press. By permission of the publisher.
12. "The Roles of Teacher and Critic," from the *Journal of General Education*, XXII, 1, 1970, pp. 41-49.

Preface

In preparing this collection for publication, I have selected from my published articles those which seemed to me of most interest to practising teachers. I hope that this book may encourage teachers to reflect on their aims and methods, and that it may provide some of the tools to assist them. The introduction is new, and is designed to explain the nature of the work undertaken in the subsequent chapters, and also to anticipate a number of objections which may be expected to arise. My approach to conceptual analysis has been very much influenced by the published work of Alan White and Antony Flew and I am happy to acknowledge my indebtedness.

I have edited the individual articles in order to introduce uniformity, to improve style, and to eliminate dated references. In places, particularly in Chapter Eleven, I have made certain changes in the argument. The notes have been revised to bring them up to date, to supply certain cross references in the text, and to add further references.

It is a great pleasure to see these articles, which appeared over a period of a decade in a wide variety of journals in Canada and abroad, now gathered in more accessible form. I wish to thank the various editors of the journals in which the articles originally appeared for permission to republish them in this book. I am very grateful to The Althouse Press for its co-operation in producing this collection.

Prior to publication, many of the papers were delivered at seminars and conferences: Chapter One was read at the Department of Educational Foundations, Memorial University, in March 1972; Chapter Three was presented at the Philosophy Department seminar, University of Hull, England, in October 1976; Chapter Four was given at the C.S.S.E. meetings in Quebec City, June 1976; Chapter Six was originally prepared as a discussion paper for the Canada Studies Foundation; Chapter Eight was presented at the

Atlantic Regional Philosophy conference, Acadia University, in March 1975; Chapter Nine was read at the Atlantic Education Association conference, University of Prince Edward Island, November 1972; Chapter Eleven was a contribution to the C.S.S.E. meetings at Queen's University, in June 1973. I wish to thank all those who commented at the time, with particular thanks to David Braybrooke who offered valuable suggestions about a number of the papers, and to Bruce Roald who invited me to prepare the paper on cultural diversity.

Finally, I am very grateful to Thérèse Boutilier for typing the manuscript, and to my wife Niki for proofreading it and for suggesting the project originally.

Table of Contents

	Page
PREFACE	(vii)
INTRODUCTION	1

Part One - Slogans in Education
1. Learning: Experience and Enjoyment — 13
2. The Criterion of Relevance — 19
3. The Concept of Innovation in Education — 27
4. Calling a Halt: Comments on John Holt's *Escape from Childhood* — 39

Part Two - Aims
5. Appreciation as a Goal of Aesthetic Education — 53
6. Education Amid Cultural Diversity — 61
7. Education and Cultural Disadvantage — 71

Part Three - Teacher Education
8. Teaching: Preparation and Certification — 79
9. Models of Field Experience — 89
10. Philosophy as a Vocational Handicap — 99

Part Four - The Role of the Teacher
11. Controversial Issues and the Teacher — 109
12. The Roles of Teacher and Critic — 121

Notes — 131

Introduction

The Nature and Value of Philosophy of Education

Often dismissed as interesting but irrelevant, philosophy of education has in fact a distinctive and vital contribution to make to our understanding of education. And such understanding has an important bearing on practice. Disillusionment sets in when philosophy is expected to provide answers to questions which fall outside its scope. Or when the questions which it can deal with are regarded as trivial. Philosophers are themselves largely to blame for the widespread disenchantment on both counts. In the first place, philosophers of education have often claimed to be able to derive all manner of detailed, practical recommendations from some general philosophical position.[1] The mistake here is that of viewing philosophy as a kind of *superscience* which can dispense with the findings of psychology and sociology. The distinctive role of philosophy in educational theory is lost. In the second place, however, many who recognize the sorts of questions which philosophy can tackle, go on to argue that these are unimportant, empty and narrow.[2] But to recognize the limited role that philosophy has to play compared with the total role of a *superscience* is not to say that the limited role is unimportant or irrelevant. In fact, the careful examination of educational concepts and theories which characterizes philosophy of education is a necessary condition of any serious attempt to deal with educational issues.

1. Conceptual Analysis: Its Richness And Diversity

The catchall title usually given to the dominant form of contemporary philosophy of education is *conceptual analysis*, but this expression is hardly self-explanatory. It is badly, one suspects sometimes deliberately, misinterpreted by those who dismiss it as "dictionary dabbling," playing with words, or bowing down before ordinary language. In fact, it has nothing to do with finding synonyms, being interested rather in trying to bring out those features which are necessary to the idea in question. The pejorative "playing with words" fails to do justice to the serious search for an understanding of those important concepts or ideas which we use our words to capture. And ordinary language is no arbiter in these matters, for it can be seriously misleading. What is true, however, is that we can often pick up important clues about a concept by noticing that something or other cannot sensibly be said. We learn something about what it is to know or have knowledge when we recognize that we cannot properly say that we *knew* something but it was *false*.

"Conceptual analysis" serves as a generic label to cover a number of different, if related, activities.[3] The ultimate purpose of these activities is to discover what is *necessarily* true of our concepts as opposed to what is *accidentally* so. For example, it happens to be the case that, in this part of the world, education is expensive. But it is obviously true that this does not tell us anything about the idea of education itself. A necessary truth about education would be something which could not be denied without contradiction. And this is why philosophy can, to some extent, be an armchair pursuit. If, however, it is to be *applied* in any serious and useful way, conceptual claims must be combined with factual claims derived from empirical research.

There is then a single, overriding objective in analysis, the identification of necessary truths. But this objective is pursued in a great variety of ways. I make no attempt here to give anything like a complete catalogue of tasks which analysis takes on. The following examples, drawn from the chapters which follow, are merely illustrative of some of the more important jobs to be tackled in conceptual analysis. These are more than sufficient, however, to show that any simplistic view of analysis is inadequate.

(i) In asking, for example, how we ought to think of practice teaching, we can usefully begin by sorting out as many *plausible* categories as possible. Unless we sketch out a wide range of possible perspectives, our recommendation will be based on an inadequate and possibly distorted sample. Part of our task here will involve trying to *formulate* a clear concept of field experience for this is a newly coined term whose conceptual boundaries are far from clear. Ordinary usage is not very helpful, since the idea is just gaining currency.

(ii) One danger, however, in setting out such a range of possible categories is the temptation to conclude too quickly that there are several *senses* of the concept in question.[4] For example, there are many different ways in which people can be disadvantaged, but are there several senses of this concept? Analysis probes further to discover if possible that root notion which links apparently different senses. In this way, we may begin to appreciate, just what a disadvantage is, which is different from knowing that it takes this or that form.

(iii) We may, of course, discover that what we at first took to be a single thing, for example, *the* aim of education in the context of cultural diversity, must be recognized as a shorthand reference to several, logically distinct, aims. It will be important here to chart such logical differences carefully, for, in recognizing these, we will be in a better position to find out how best to try to achieve the aims in question. Philosophy, of course, does not directly answer this methodological issue, but it serves to bring the question into sharper relief.

(iv) Having shown that what is apparently one thing must be subdivided into distinct parts, we can nevertheless ask what, if any, are the logical connections between, or among, these parts. In the context of separate, though related, aims, is it the case that one such aim must logically be met before some other can be sought? More generally, we can search for the logical implications of an idea which link it with other ideas. In doing this, we are trying to develop a *theory* of how the concept operates. Recommendations for practice often rest on false claims, or false assumptions, about logical relationships among concepts, such as the claim, or assumption, that experience and enjoyment are *sufficient* conditions of education. Analysis examines such claims, or unearths such assumptions, in order to test the alleged connection.

(v) Since the philosopher's concern is with what is necessarily true, it is clear that analysis will be very concerned to examine *arguments* for their validity. The task here involves, among other things, the detection of fallacies, the

4 / Controversies in Teaching

exposure of mere rhetoric, the recognition of ambiguity, and the denunciation of unsupported assertion. In the chapters devoted to the ideas of John Holt and Herbert Kohl, I show how elementary points of informal logic are helpful in assessing educational proposals.

(vi) An interest in logical properties can help us to bring out the *significance* of a logical feature, when its obviousness may disguise its importance. We may be clear, for example, about the general meaning of relevance, but noticing that it is a *relational* concept is at once to recognize that the *simple* assertion that something is, or is not, relevant, conceals any reference to that which would establish the claim. What is concealed in the deceptively simple claim may contain a host of assumptions about the nature and purpose of education, assumptions which might soon run into difficulty if exposed to criticism.

(vii) Analysis can often reveal that value judgments are lurking in what appear to be descriptive claims. It is important, for example, to bring out the fact that the notion of innovation is value-laden, for this serves to remind us that there is an obligation to show how the proposed change is educationally valuable.

(viii) Interestingly, the previous move can be reversed, for at times aspects of apparently contentious value issues can be seen to reduce to conceptual points. We may dispute the value of teaching history at all; but if we are to teach history in a way which avoids distortion of the subject matter then *as a matter of logic* controversial issues must come up. The fact is that serious historians do dispute evidence and interpretation.

(ix) A creative task for analysis involves employing what might be termed the *instructive contrast*. Two distinct concepts are brought into juxtaposition, with the result that each is seen in a new perspective. Even if our primary interest is in the question "what is law?", it may be better *not* to ask this question but rather "How is law different from commands?"[5] The contrast points the way to a fuller understanding. Such a move is developed at length in the chapter which contrasts the roles of teacher and critic.

(x) Finally, we might mention that general task, illustrated in different ways in the various chapters in this book, of reminding us of the *limits* of our knowledge. We come to realize that a claim is vague, obscure or confused. We see that a certain sort of claim cannot *in principle* be established in a certain way. We are forced to admit that we simply do not have an argument for something we nevertheless still believe in. In these and other ways, analysis can begin that process of self-awareness, which, as Socrates realized, is the beginning of wisdom.

2. *Objections and Replies*

It is clear then that analysis is altogether more complex and searching than its detractors would allow. In sketching its nature in the preceding section, I have inevitably hinted from time to time at the value of analytical philosophy. Though the value of the essays in this book will have to be tested in the experience of individual teachers who read them, it may be possible to bring out the value of analysis in a general way by reviewing some common complaints.

(i) It is very often alleged that philosophy of education is of no practical value. This is an important criticism to answer, because it is not sufficient to maintain that philosophy is valuable in itself. The latter point is correct but irrelevant in the context of teacher education. In the limited time available in teacher education programs, it is surely necessary to select courses which contribute to a person's development *as a teacher.*

The doubt arises because conceptual analysis is an abstract and theoretical business, and this is contrasted with the practical nature of classroom teaching. The crucial reply is this. Practice is itself enmeshed in theory, for our practice reveals the way in which we think of teaching, and the kinds of criteria we draw on in making pedagogical decisions. But then our view of teaching may be narrow and constraining, and our criteria may be far removed from central educational concerns. If our practice shows that our *unexamined* theory is that teaching can be summed up as "experience and enjoyment," then our practice is based on an impoverished view of education.

(ii) It may be further objected that there is no reason why a teacher *must* fall into such a view and that many teachers, who know nothing of conceptual analysis, have taught in a way which reflects a rich and fruitful concept of education. This must surely be admitted but it does nothing to weaken the claim that conceptual analysis has an important bearing on educational issues and that teachers can profit from studying analysis.[6]

(iii) Many who would be prepared to concede the points just made are nevertheless concerned about the controversial nature of philosophy. Reservations have often taken the form of suggesting that nothing is ever *settled* in philosophy. Again, there is enough truth behind this remark to forestall any casual dismissal. If the philosophers are in disagreement, the teacher must nevertheless get on with the task at hand. The practice of teaching cannot await the solution of theoretical disputes. Moreover, if the teacher turns to philosophy and finds controversy, what practical advice can be gleaned?

If, however, we encounter serious disputes about the aims of education, we may surely learn to appreciate the intractable nature of such questions, and thereby develop an appropriate humility with respect to any answer we adopt. Teachers can come to recognize the importance of keeping such questions open, when others are anxious to close them in arbitrary and objectionable ways.[7] Moreover, although such issues may not admit of final answers, nevertheless we can become clearer about the utter inadequacy of certain proposed answers. Here things *can* be settled. It can no longer seriously be claimed, for example, that an educational curriculum can be based in any simple way on the study of what interests a child. Yet simplistic solutions have been enormously influential, as can be seen in connection with John Holt's ideas, and it is vital that philosophy expose the shortcomings in these answers.

(iv) It is also objected that in looking at concepts such as open-mindedness, creativity and critical reflection, analysis is concentrating on *ideal* notions, and ignoring the realities and possibilities in the average classroom. Certainly, it is true that it is beside the point to recommend a course of action which is impossible. "Ought" presupposes "can." But the point of recognizing what is involved in an educational ideal is to indicate directions to be pursued where possible. It is when we have a clear concept of an educational ideal that we are able to see how far our own practice, for whatever reason, falls short of the standard. If we remain clear in our own minds that we are articulating a general goal or direction, there is no reason why the inquiry should involve self-deception, where we fondly believe that the ideal is actually being achieved.[8]

(v) A rather different criticism is that analysis is inherently *conservative* because it merely spells out what is built into our concepts, and these inevitably reflect the culture in which they occur. In analyzing the concept of education then, we are simply bringing out what is *regarded as* education in our own society, but deceive ourselves into thinking that we are somehow getting clearer about *the* concept of education. We merely reinforce our own culturally-relative conception. Against this, it must be pointed out that in fact philosophers sometimes engage in formulating a new concept. It is when analysis makes clear the limited view of teacher preparation implied by teacher *training* or *practice teaching* that the ideas of teacher *education* and *field experience* come to be developed. When we grasp the implications of an idea, we may want to abandon it. Far from being conservative in character, analysis can provoke fundamental criticism of our existing practices if, for example, we discover that our teaching too closely resembles indoctrination. There is no reason why we cannot continue to ask if there are limitations in our view of education.

(vi) It is perhaps easy to conclude that philosophers simply dodge the substantive issues, and retreat to a discussion about words. Often, a philosopher will not directly address the substantive issue, but will, for example, sort out various ambiguities or confusions inherent in the way the issue is presented. And this can seem feeble and evasive compared with a forthright stand on the question. But two comments need to be made in mitigation. In the first place, it may not be possible to tackle the issue head-on, simply because the central concepts employed are far from clear. An analysis which shows more clearly what the issue is, or what kind of issue is involved, may clear the way for a resolution. Secondly, it is simply not true that philosophers *always* avoid the substantive issue. Having clarified the notion of a controversial issue below, I go on to argue in favor of teachers including such issues and taking a stand on them.

(vii) Teachers who are familiar with influential ideas in contemporary sociology of education may be inclined to accuse the philosopher of being naïve. In searching for rational justification, the philosopher neglects the point that educational decisions are inescapably *political*. Far better then for teachers to become aware of the political nature of schooling than to concern themselves with a vain search for rational standards. So effective has the sloganizing been in this area that an attempt to question the claim here is to invite ridicule. And yet, it can be shown, I think, that the charge of naïveté is misdirected.

If the claim above is taken to mean that one's concept of education influences and reflects one's view of the good society, the point can be admitted. This does not, however, affect the *relative* distinction between a curriculum based primarily on educational rather than political considerations, and certainly does not show that political *bias* must be at work. The concepts of education and politics cannot be the same, because we can say that a policy is politically astute but educationally unwise. It is, therefore, important for analysis to try to keep clear distinctions which are in danger of being eroded.

(viii) The well-known complaint that analytical philosophy is overly intellectual and ignores emotions can also be answered. First, it would not be rational to ignore the feelings of those affected by our actions, for these too are consequences which need to be taken into account. Secondly, the gulf suggested between reason and emotion is unreal, for it is perfectly possible and sensible to ask if our emotional response to a situation is *appropriate*. Reflection on *what it is* we are proposing to do may itself prompt a powerful emotional response.

(ix) One criticism, which is as old as philosophy itself, is simply that analysis serves to make things more confusing. Where once we had a rule or principle, philosophy raises a host of doubts, qualifications and possibilities. But what exactly could this complaint be? Is it that we have had to abandon a clear but faulty rule? We are bound to ask why it should be suggested that we are worse off for having identified its shortcomings.

(x) Finally, we may consider the objection that, in its concern to analyze concepts and root out ambiguity and confusion, philosophy misses the *insights* which are contained in educational theories. Certainly, this danger must be admitted, for a theory may contain an excellent idea presented in a confused way. In fact, analytical philosophers have been concerned to call attention to this. For example, in showing that a slogan, taken literally, involves a contradiction, it is important to ask if it nevertheless manages to make an important moral point, or brings attention to an aspect of teaching which is neglected. The fact is, however, that in asking this, we are employing a distinction between literal meaning and heuristic value. It is by attending to our concepts that the nature and value of such a distinction becomes clear. Let us pursue this point immediately in Part One by examining a number of influential slogans in recent educational theory.

Notes for the Introduction: page 131

Part One
Slogans in Education

Chapter 1

Learning: Experience and Enjoyment

A complex relationship exists among the group of concepts listed in the title of this chapter such that a succinct answer to such a question as "Does learning entail experience?" is not possible. Each of the concepts admits of a number of interpretations, and I hope to indicate some of these and to suggest certain links. On the other hand, a student-teacher beginning to read around in contemporary educational theory could be forgiven for concluding that the relationship involved here is the essence of simplicity: to learn is to experience, and such experiences should be enjoyable. Here, for example, is a teacher explaining the rationale behind a field trip:

> Purpose of the trip was to give the boys as many new experiences as possible . . . . On another occasion, we drove round a traffic circle near Niagara Falls because they simply had never experienced or travelled around a traffic circle before. We travelled on the subway to the hockey game just for the experience.[1]

In this discussion the enjoyable nature of the trip is not explicitly stated though the connection with enjoyment is very clearly implied. However, it is not difficult to find the simple connection between experience and enjoyment explicitly defended:

> The child must have variety. A teacher who can get a class of children to *enjoy* their English periods with him, by whatever methods, achieves his aim.[2]

My purpose is not to convince anyone that this view is dominant in contemporary educational theory, but something like this simple view is popular, and in view of this my purposes are twofold. First, I will argue that the conceptual connections here are intricate. Secondly, from the point of view of philosophy of education I will show that the view under criticism here is importantly wrong in that it contains undesirable implications for educational practice.

1. Experience

When we say that someone has experience, we may imply that the person has knowledge gained by direct personal participation in some activity. Industry complains that university graduates have theoretical knowledge but little knowledge in the sense of experience. But this cannot be the sense of experience which educational theorists have in mind when they assert that experience is necessary for learning, because if experience means knowledge, then learning has *already* taken place. Rather, educational theorists mean by experience the direct observation or participation *itself* which results in the acquisition of knowledge. If this is how to interpret the claim, then it would seem to be false that experience is necessary for learning to take place. Consider, for example, the practice of head-hunting, which few of us have directly observed or personally participated in. Still it is clear that we understand what the practice involves. Great novelists, like George Eliot, have been able to express in their writing a vast range of feelings and emotions; and there is no reason to suppose that the novelist has personally experienced the emotions which her novel clearly depicts. Moreover, the reader can come to understand the nature of an emotion such as extreme jealousy, though it is foreign to his nature and he has never experienced it. I am not, of course, denying that reading a novel is an experience. But there is a difference between directly experiencing an emotion and reading about a character who displays a certain emotion.

If the aim of an educational institution is to promote learning of a certain kind, then a description of the purpose of any particular part of an educational program in terms of "giving new experiences" must be inadequate. This is because having experiences in the sense of direct participation is not a sufficient condition of learning anything. It is of course possible to define experience in such a way that it implies learning,[3] but then experience could not be identified with direct observation or personal participation. One could be driven around a traffic circle without learning anything, for learning here requires coming to understand a complex framework in which certain traditions, rules, and social purposes have a place. An experience can, as we say, go over a person's head, because that person is not in a position to make sense of the experience he has had.

In those cases in which direct observation does lead to learning, it does not follow that the inclusion of such an experience in an educational program is justified. It is further necessary to show that the learning which has taken place is of value. Certain uses of the term "experience" can lead one to conclude that no such additional justification is necessary. We often say, "It was an experience" and mean to suggest that the experience was valuable. After visiting a new country and coming to appreciate a different way of life a person might say "It was an experience." The context would clearly imply that he regarded the trip as valuable. I do not want to deny that visiting a traffic circle may be valuable in a similar way, but rather the point is that the expression "just for the experience" is a dangerous oversimplification. Certain experiences may not be valuable at all, for example, being viciously attacked on a city street. It is, of course, possible that a person might learn something of value from such an experience, but no one would propose such an experience as part of an educational program. Part of the educator's responsibility is to select among possible experiences, and this possibility is neglected if we speak of doing an action just for the experience.

2. *Enjoyment*

Consideration of such a counter-example brings out an inconsistency in the oversimplified connection between experience and enjoyment. All experiences are not enjoyable. A person who survives a plane crash could sensibly say: "What an experience! I never want to go through that again." Thus, at the level of consistency, qualifications have to be entered against the simple formula, for if learning is to be enjoyable, certain experiences will have to be eliminated. But it is necessary to examine the claims that enjoyment must be part of learning.

The "must" here might be (a) prescriptive or (b) logical.

16 / Controversies in Teaching

Considering the logical claim, it cannot be maintained that enjoyment is a necessary condition of learning. Many students intensely dislike certain subjects but achieve some degree of understanding in them. While they are learning they would deny that they enjoy the work. Nor is it the case that when they come to learn they necessarily enjoy the subject. A person might be obliged to learn to skate but never come to enjoy this exercise.

Coming to the prescriptive claim, it seems difficult to maintain that all school experiences ought to be enjoyable unless it can be shown that they *can* be enjoyable. Suppose one were to find that something valuable, for example history, was not enjoyed by students and that no practical way could be found to make it enjoyable. This would not be sufficient grounds for removing the subject from the curriculum. It might be that in a given area enjoyment did not come until some measure of learning had taken place. Certain unenjoyable experiences can be learning experiences. It may not be enjoyable to learn that a piece of work is illogical, poorly argued, and so on, yet a student can learn and profit from such an experience.

Enjoyment is not a necessary condition of learning though it may be desirable to make our lessons as enjoyable as possible. But it would be a mistake to think that making them enjoyable ensured that (a) learning or (b) education were taking place. All enjoyable experiences do not lead to learning. For example, a student may be entertained or amused by a teacher without learning taking place. In those cases where the enjoyable experience does produce learning, it does not follow that what is learned is of educational value. The learning may be trivial (spelling words backwards) or immoral (making counterfeit money). Learning may be taking place though nothing of educational value is occurring.

It is sometimes claimed that a person could not be said to understand a discipline such as history unless he regards it as worthwhile.[4] I think there is a clear use of the term "enjoy" in our language from which it follows that if a person regards history as worthwhile he enjoys it. However, it seems false to claim that *understanding* demands as a necessary condition that the person regard the activity as worthwhile. To regard history as worthwhile is not to know any more history, nor

Learning: Experience and Enjoyment / 17

to understand better what one already knows; it is to view what one knows in a different light. What seems to be true, however, is that a person would not be called educated, or an educated historian, if he did not regard the subject as worthwhile. Thus, it would be conceptually odd to maintain that an educated historian did not enjoy his subject. This, of course, is quite different from saying that he experiences pleasurable feelings in all aspects of his work as an historian. Aspects of his work may be exhausting, tedious, and dull but none of this would imply that he did not enjoy his work.

Notes for Chapter One: page 131

Chapter 2

The Criterion of Relevance

Some words, like "racist," excite such horror, and others like "human rights" provoke such fervent enthusiasm, that it is difficult at times to persuade ourselves that we should pause to examine what these terms mean or to wonder whether charges against people in connection with these ideas are really warranted in a particular case. If we stop to query whether or not Arthur Jensen has been fairly accused of racism, it may seem that we ourselves are dabbling with that evil, so we had better be against it. If we make a distinction between the honest publication of research findings which others might use for racist purposes and the fabrication of research findings for avowed racist purposes, we are muddying up the water—our opposition must be firm and absolute. Now as foolish as this may seem when considered rationally, an examination of some of the things which are said on occasion forces one to the conclusion that otherwise reasonable people cannot think rationally about certain topics, particularly those which they care about very much. "Relevance" is I think, such a word in the context of educational theory. To ask, as I shall do here, what it means and why it is important may be regarded as redundant or dangerous. But since so much hinges on one's view that a course is relevant or irrelevant, it is vital that we have a clear account of the concept. We can become so accustomed to regarding a particular course as irrelevant that we lose sight of the *grounds* on which such a charge is justified. There is the danger too that people will cease to consider whether or not their classes really are irrelevant, in case it should appear that they are not sufficiently committed to the watchword. But then of course, some classes which *are* relevant will be abandoned for no good reason. Finally there is the unnerving possibility that courses might be assessed on grounds other than their relevance or lack of it.

1. General Features of the Term

It is, in the first place, a relational term. A thing cannot be relevant or irrelevant *per se* or in itself, but only in relation to something else. If that other thing disappears or ceases to concern us, what was once relevant may become irrelevant. Connected with this is the point that the concept is very much context-dependent. X may be relevant to Y in certain circumstances only. Knowledge of a person's motives are usually relevant in determining liability, but in cases of strict liability motives are irrelevant. It is, further, a relationship among ideas. Comments, suggestions, remarks, programs and criticism are among the sorts of things which can be relevant or irrelevant. A person (as opposed to a person's opinions, for example) cannot be said to be relevant or irrelevant; nor can an object (as opposed to a suggestion about an object), though it can be useful or important. Something, then, like a car, can be important but not relevant. Conversely, something can be relevant to something else but not regarded as important because that to which it is relevant is not valued. If on such occasions we say that the suggestion is irrelevant, this involves substituting some other end or goal in relation to which we want the suggestion considered, unless of course we merely wish to deny the facts. It may be that we think the other person is just *mistaken* in taking something to be relevant to another thing. We do not quarrel with the end-state, but query the alleged relevance of something to it. Thus, disputes in this area may be value disputes or factual in nature. In connection with factual disputes, however, it is only rarely that it is a plain matter of fact, for example, like the view that the study of education is relevant to the practice of teaching. Often, the view that something is or is not relevant calls for careful *judgment*. Whether or not X has a bearing on Y is not written into things. It calls for human decision, and it is quite possible not to notice a connection which in fact exists.

2. An Educational Example

The study of the classics has in many places almost entirely vanished from the school curriculum, and not infrequently the disappearance is explained and justified in terms of an alleged lack of relevance. But the relational nature of the concept is rarely recognized, for what it is that the classics lack relevance *to* is not mentioned. End-states like "the modern world" are worse than useless in this context, for being vague in the extreme they merely give us the illusion of having thought the problem through. What *precisely* is it about the modern context which would justify such a judgment? Since it is a judgment, ability to declare the classics irrelevant demands experience, knowledge, skill and expertise. This is not the kind of view which is a plain matter of fact. Unless the end-state is spelled out in some detail, we cannot decide what importance to attach to the claim that the classics are or are not relevant, because it might be true that they are relevant to a goal which would be regarded as educationally insignificant. We cannot, however tempting, opt for the view that the individual is necessarily the best judge of his own situation, because he may not have noticed or recognized how the classics are relevant to an end-state which he himself values. Or he may dismiss them as irrelevant according to a very limited concept of education, for example, what will get him a job. A person can only claim immunity for the statement "It's irrelevant for me," if we assume that he is always the best judge of what is in his educational interests. The general features discussed in Section 1 clearly produce a host of complex questions which are presupposed in any charge of irrelevancy. My worry about the disappearance of the classics does not relate to the answers which have been given to these questions, but to the fact that the questions have not been raised.

3. Some Sources of Irrelevancy
Consideration of the same general features can help us to understand some of the ways in which irrelevancy can enter into school curricula.
(i) The very idea of schooling may seem to be irrelevant to some groups, such as the disadvantaged, because the quality of their lives will not be improved by this institution. (In some cases, their very view that the institution will not improve their lives may mean that indeed it will not help them.) For example, the school may try to transmit a concern for others, for the principles of justice. But the environment in which some of the disadvantaged live may make such prin-

ciples useless. David Hume, the eighteenth-century philosopher, suggested that it would be foolish for a man to try to follow principles of justice if he fell in with a band of ruffians.[1] This is merely to show that principles which are valuable in one context may be without value in another. But the present context is not necessarily *unalterable*. What is needed surely are fundamental social changes such that the principles of justice are not useless and irrelevant. It may be too that otherwise valuable activities will have to be suspended from the curriculum until the social context is sufficiently altered to make it feasible to include them again.

(ii) Evaluation becomes irrelevant if an inappropriate standard is adopted. One's overall enjoyment of a student's essay may be marred because it is presented late, in messy form, with serious misspellings and so on, but none of these criteria is relevant to an assessment of the *literary* worth which it may have. Similarly, the style of a sentence has no bearing on the truth of the claim which the sentence makes. As teachers then, we need to be quite clear about the criteria of success in any area of education in order to eliminate criticism and failure based on irrelevant matters.

(iii) Irrelevancy is a constant threat in teaching simply because activities like history and science have built-in ground rules which define the activity. In this way, guessing becomes irrelevant because it is not an appropriate procedure, though I am not saying that there is never a place for an educated guess. In conversation with friends, it is much harder, though not impossible, to say something irrelevant than in a discussion because conversation is much more open and flexible; the ground rules are loose and vague and consequently not so easily violated.

(iv) An overemphasis on theory to the neglect of practice and experience is often criticized not in terms of an imbalance but in terms of irrelevancy. Very often theory may not be relevant either to what the practice is or to what it should be. Here, of course, what one needs is better theory not an elimination of theory. Equally often, however, the complaint is really that the relevance of the theory is not apparent or seen. The different complaints "This is irrelevant" and "I cannot *see* the relevance of this" are not always sufficiently distinguished in our thinking. Relevancy, to parody justice, not only ought to exist, it ought to be seen to exist. This states an ideal, however, because in reality one cannot always see the relevance of something until much later. It is for this reason that the answer to the question "Why study this?" cannot at times be grasped until one has studied it to some extent.

(v) We live at a time when "the explosion of knowledge" is already a well-worn cliché, but the truth in the phrase clearly underlines a further potential source of irrelevancy. This is peculiarly acute in certain disciplines like science and history where material can "date" so quickly. (It would be interesting to pursue the question why literature and philosophy, for example, do not suffer to the same extent from this phenomenon.) A related danger is that we discuss "problems" which are just not central enough to the important questions which bother students. Moral philosophers used to delight in discussions of cases such as "Would it be wrong not to pay your bus fare if you had a chance to get away with it?" It does not take much reflection to see that this hardly gets to the heart of serious moral dilemmas, and often in class we side-step the serious in this way. A further aspect of the same problem is the fact that we cannot know in some cases what our teaching is supposed to be relevant to. What will the student need to know in ten years' time, or the student-teacher in two years' time? There is an element of uncertainty here which makes a certain amount of irrelevancy almost inevitable.

(vi) Too often, the schools have ignored the real needs of students. A student may need an opportunity to study aspects of his own cultural group, free from bias and prejudice, to speak and use his native language, free from criticism and social handicap, if he is to develop a secure sense of his own worth.[2] And no one should grow up without the latter. Relevant aspects will be ignored if we operate with some such goal as "initiation into the dominant culture." It is, of course, a complete dodge (as others, e.g., John Passmore,[3] have shown) to say that there isn't time to do anything else. This masquerades as a comfortable factual judgment whereas it is in reality a disguised value judgment for it is only the case that there "isn't time" if there are other things which we consider more important.

4. The Limits of Relevance

In the practical context of teaching, many comments made by students in class are just not relevant to the question at issue. They may, of course, be very interesting in themselves but, for all that, are irrelevant if they have no bearing on the issue. Let us suppose a case in which an irrelevant comment is not at all interesting and indeed reveals a mistaken view of the subject; still, there may be pedagogical grounds for giving it an airing. Apart from the fact that the statement of an irrelevant point may indicate more precisely where relevance lies, refusal to listen may prevent any points (relevant *or* irrelevant) from being raised in the future. Every teacher knows this instinctively, but it serves to show that relevance is not our only, nor our most important, value.

Because it is a relational concept, relevance always points to something else, but educational activities can be regarded as having *intrinsic* value, i.e. they are valuable in and for themselves. They can be pursued for their own sake, and not merely because they lead on to something else. Can we ask, for example, of a piece of music "What is its relevance?" In certain contexts, of course, we can. If two people are having a philosophical argument and one says "Listen" and plays a piece of music, the other is surely entitled to ask how that is supposed to be relevant. But the question does not always make sense. Some music is simply worth listening to, and is neither relevant nor irrelevant to anything else that we may want. The question of its relevance just does not arise. It is simply worthwhile. And, to return to our classics example, it may be (and I think it is) the case that an understanding of an ancient civilization is worthwhile in itself quite apart from questions about its relevance to any other understanding.

This is basically the point made by Bertrand Russell when he noted with regret in *In Praise of Idleness and Other Essays:*

> "About 100 years ago, a number of well-meaning philanthropists started societies 'for the diffusion of useful knowledge' with the result that people have ceased to appreciate the delicious savour of 'useless' knowledge."

The Criterion of Relevance / 25

And even David Hume, the arch defender of utility in matters of value, took pains to point out that some qualities are "immediately agreeable."[4]

Notes for Chapter Two: pages 131-132

Chapter 3

The Concept of Innovation in Education

All things flow by, thought Heraclitus, but many educational thinkers wish that schooling practices flowed by somewhat faster. The cry for change[1] has now joined the familiar chorus which demands relevance and openness. It is not easy for the practising teacher to raise a lone query about the implications of this demand, but it is both natural and necessary for philosophers of education to do so. Natural, because the question is essentially philosophical, as a demand to know what is meant, and why it is thought to be a good thing; and necessary, if educational policies are to be based on rational and critical inquiry. Fortunately, philosophers of education have already entered this area,[2] and thus my comments should be seen as a contribution to a debate underway.

1. Change and Innovation

It has been persuasively argued by Pratte that change is a necessary but not a sufficient condition of innovation.[3] He suggests as a further necessary condition that the change be the result of human purposing rather than an accident or a case of natural development. Pratte does not, however, describe this necessary condition in unambiguous terms, for "the degree of human purposing displayed in the situation" covers both 1) the case in which X acts intentionally and produces a change, though he was unaware of the novelty in his production, and 2) the case in which X acts intentionally *to* change something. I suspect that Pratte has sense 2) in mind, though it may be that he purposely left the description ambiguous. In any case, it is worth noting that we would not exclude 1) from the concept of innovation. If X, who is ignorant of the history of *art*, intentionally produces a painting (of great originality), it cannot be the case that he had intended to change accepted form, style, and so on (for he had no knowledge of these), and yet his work would properly be called innovative.[4]

Finally, Pratte suggests that it is further necessary that the change be judged "sufficiently different" before we can speak of an innovation. Not every change will be regarded as a sufficiently significant departure from what went before to warrant calling it an innovation. This makes the ascription of the term "innovative" essentially a comparative activity, undertaken in a certain context. The claim that the ascription "innovative" involves a judgment should not be confused with the claim that it involves a value judgment, for we can say that X is significantly different from Y without saying that it is better or worse than Y. The non-value judgment presupposes familiarity with, and understanding of, the area in which the judgment is made.[5]

It is important to bear in mind the kind of judgment which is involved here, because Pratte wishes to hold that a value judgment is not necessarily implied by the term "innovation." It is probably more accurate to summarize Pratte's view by saying that he holds that the concept of innovation is not necessarily value-laden, rather than by saying that it is for him necessarily value-neutral. He does, after all, admit that *sometimes the concept does imply alteration for the better.*

Certainly, it is true that, etymologically, there is no necessary link with a value-judgment; and in historical usage no such conceptual connection has existed. It was Burke, I believe, who insisted that to innovate was not necessarily to reform. Still, the fact that such a comment needed to be made should give us cause to ponder, for it may indicate a refusal to sanction a conceptual revision which was occurring. Such revision has occurred when a term comes to be used in new or altered manner, although there remains a significant overlap with former usage.[6] It seems to me that we now use the term "innovation" in accordance with the three criteria outlined by Pratte [i.e., 1) a purposeful, 2) change, 3) of some significance] but with the further implication that the change is a change which we value to some extent. It is now essentially a *value-laden* term, the use of which necessarily involves a judgment of positive worth. We do not use it for a significant change which we regard as a regression.

Pratte does, however, present one apparent counterexample,[7] and it is on the basis of this case that he concludes

The Concept of Innovation in Education / 29

that "innovation" sometimes expresses *disapproval*. Asking what comes to mind when the term "educational innovation" is used, Pratte suggests one possible response might be: "Oh, you mean those damn 'mini-courses' they are putting into the high school, I'm sure glad my daughter is out of that place." On the face of it, this does suggest disapproval, but I think the counterexample can be accommodated in the following manner. Surely, this is an example of what has come to be termed "external, descriptive" or even "inverted commas" usage,[8] where the person is really saying something like "This is the sort of thing some educational theorists call innovation, but I don't!"—where the "scare quotes" show that he is not using the term in its usual way. It is, I think, not far removed from that kind of sarcasm in which a term is deliberately employed when it is believed to be inappropriate.[9]

Pratte does not sufficiently distinguish 1) the judgment that X is better than Y, and 2) the judgment that X is of some value. He says that the term "educational innovation" is "sometimes mixed, serving both to describe and evaluate"[10] and further that it is only sometimes the case that the term implies an *improvement*. It seems to me that whereas the latter claim is true, the former is false. Certainly, a new and ingenious surgical procedure could be called an innovation, even if it were no better than some existing procedure. But if a change is either of *no value* or judged to be of *disvalue*, we would not speak of an innovation. Thus, it is not the case that the concept of "innovation" is sometimes mixed, for it is always the case that descriptive and evaluative claims are involved, though not necessarily the evaluative claim that it constitutes an improvement.

We have found it useful to employ a term which, unlike the value-neutral word "change," suggests that the change is valuable. Of course, the judgment of value expressed in the word "innovation" does not guarantee that the new practice will live up to our expectations. It expresses our belief in the positive value of the change, but it is always possible that this belief is ill-founded. This further confuses the descriptive-evaluative issue, for X, which is justifiably called an innovation, may turn out to be without value or even disastrous. But this does not offset the claim that when X is deemed to be an innovation, it is thought to be a desirable or valuable change. In much the same way, claims to knowledge are often defeated.

It is not implied by the term that the practice is quite original in the way that a first-time scientific discovery is. We need to recall that the term is used in a comparative way. Thus, it was innovative in the recent history of schooling when teachers and students started moving outside the classroom into the community, although this had been done before in other contexts.[11] But it can be judged here as sufficiently different from a pattern of instruction which had become entrenched. Acupuncture, when approved, will be an innovation in Western medical practice, though it is an ancient art. This point is not well recognized. A recent book states: "Forty innovations are treated here. Some of them might more properly be called revivals rather than innovations."[12] This falsely suggests that the two concepts are mutually exclusive.

2. The Educational Context

(i) Change for Its Own Sake

Armed with the distinction between "change" and "innovation" outlined above, it is clearly important to be critical of educational theorists who treat the terms synonymously or who blur the distinction.[13] It is a conceptual truth that an innovation is of value and a commonplace that change is not always in a desirable direction. A patient's condition changes when it worsens as well as when it improves. We normally need to know a good deal more about the situation, in addition to the fact that it constitutes a change, before we can say whether it is desirable or not. We do not think there is a presumption in favor of change, as there might be, say, in favor of freedom; or a presumption against change, as there might be against indoctrination. It just seems to be neutral, possibly good or possibly bad depending upon the circumstances. Hence we are properly skeptical of banners and slogans which assert that "Continuing change is needed."

Before leaving this point, however, it is well to recognize cases in which "change for its own sake" is reasonable and understandable, in order to be clear about the limits of these. There seem to be at least two sorts of cases in which a person could reasonably desire change, period: 1) it is just a change that he wants so as to break the monotony of some activity or life-style; 2) any change is welcome, not because it is different, but being different it will in fact improve the condition of his life.

Consider this second case. It is possible to regard a state of affairs as being so terrible that any change would be better than none at all. This is, of course, in general a dangerous principle to adopt, because it may be that our limited imagination did not conceive how the state of affairs might be worse, or that we have failed to notice, or have forgotten, the valuable features of the present state. We would have to be quite certain that the situation could not be any worse, before any change would be welcome whatever it is. This is not really a case of change for the sake of change, but a case in which any change will do because it is believed that it will in fact improve the situation. It will not improve it because it is different, but is bound to improve it because the present condition is the worst possible. This seems to me to be a principle of desperation and one which could scarcely have relevance to the educational context. The onus is quite certainly on those who would appeal to it to show that the educational situation could not be worse. Until such a case is forthcoming, the principle can be laid aside. And moreover, if *per impossibile* such a situation were to arise, alternative courses of action could still be rationally discussed. We do not have to opt for any change at all.

The first case mentioned above has some marginal relevance for the educational context. We sometimes do things "just for a change," as we say, and value the difference because it relieves the boredom we were experiencing. Without this contrast, that which constitutes "the change" might have been singularly unattractive. It is sometimes the routinely boring character of one's life which is the problem, and what is needed is something different, at least for a while. In itself, that which constitutes "the change" may not be any better or more attractive than one's routine, but the very change will improve one's lot. In the life of the school, as with life elsewhere, some variety of this kind may be desirable, but two comments must be made: 1) It is not just any change which will be welcomed, for we will often prefer to continue to be bored than to be affected in some new and undesirable way. It is only as a joke that a person would say of a spell in a hospital with a serious illness: "Well, at least it was a change!"[14] 2) The consideration of variety is subordinate to other principles which govern educational decisions. Does the change serve to promote valuable learning? Does it endanger the central task of an educational institution? Change to offset boredom invokes a psychological consideration with respect to interest and motivation, a consideration of some importance in teaching, but one which must serve more fundamental moral and educational principles. There is some danger of this truth being lost sight of by those who place paramount importance on felt-interest and entertainment in schooling. Boredom is clearly not a good in itself, but there may not be any way of removing certain boring aspects of worthwhile learning, as we noted earlier in Chapter One.

(ii) Sources of Dispute

It is, then, logically possible to be in favor of change for its own sake in the educational context, but it is only on rare occasions that this principle could be appealed to with justification. A quite different matter arises, however, when we speak of innovation, for by definition this is a change of some value. Logically, a person cannot fail to value what he accepts as an innovation, because in regarding it as an innovation he reveals that he does value it. Clearly, however, a person may wish to dispute the view that a proposal is an innovation and may well come out against "so-called innovations." The point is that despite the conceptual claim that innovation is value-laden, there remains of necessity the *substantive* question: Is it an innovation? Sophistical verbal juggling will not answer this, nor prevent it from arising. My purpose in this section is two-fold: 1) to sketch the complexities involved in making the judgment that X is an innovation and to reveal the numerous sources of dispute; 2) to suggest, as a result of this, that it is naïve and misleading to denounce others as being "against innovation." It is naïve, because it provides a simple blanket explanation for what may well be a whole variety of objections. And it is misleading because it seeks to condemn one's opponents out of hand as somehow

The Concept of Innovation in Education / 33

being, rather foolishly, opposed to what is obviously valuable. We cannot have it both ways: If we use "innovation" in a value-laden way, we must allow the claim to enter the public forum in which value judgments are assessed.

It is commonly the case that what one person is prepared to call an educational innovation, someone else will dismiss as nonsense. To some, Illich is the most innovative of educational theorists, but to others his views appear, in an engaging paradox, as "smart-silly."[15] Our earlier analysis suggests how such argument arises, but here I wish to bring out the different sorts of issues which such disputes may involve.

(a) There is, in the first place, the assertion that no *significant*[16] change has taken place. It will readily be admitted that, superficially, things seem to have changed radically, but the appearances are deceptive. Notice that the disputants here could agree that the changes are, as far as they go, of some value, but some hold that the changes are not central enough to warrant the term "innovative." The following is a very clear example. The author lists a number of features of traditional schooling and then comments: "These characteristics also apply to supposedly innovative schools; for if we are honest about it, the innovations of the past decade have resulted in at best minimal changes."[17] It does not follow that the author believes that "team-teaching," "modular-scheduling," etc. are of no value; rather he thinks that they do not get to the heart of the problems with traditional schooling.

Such disputes are sometimes conducted in language which suggests that the issue resolves around some plain matter of fact; e.g., "things have not really changed." "Yes, they have." An impasse which suggests that *observation* may settle the matter. Now observation is always relevant to such disputes, and sometimes the dispute is entirely factual, though scarcely ever is it a "plain matter of fact." But certainly the sophisticated observer may detect a change which the layperson will miss.[18] If the issue is a factual one, then more careful observation is the appropriate way to tackle it. Often, however, talk of "real change" is a disguised judgment masquerading as a plain matter of fact. "Real" is made to do the work of "significant." We must first of all then learn to avoid being bullied into accepting a view because it is presented as an "obviously true" factual remark, when it is actually a controversial assessment or interpretation. Consider here John Holt's recent statement that "Most schools have changed very little."[19] The charge is not that few changes have occurred, but rather that the changes which have occurred have not made a significant difference, because "the spirit, on the whole, is what it always was." Holt merely offers this judgment and does not attempt to back it up. It is, however, clearly of a controversial nature. What is meant here by "spirit"? What sorts of observations would be relevant in support of this assertion? Why are the changes which have occurred irrelevant to the spirit of the school? Is the central consideration, in any case, the spirit of the institution or something else, such as the aims or the methods?

The tools of analytical philosophy are invaluable in facing such disputes. One part of this enterprise is to ask which features or aspects are central to a practice, institution, or concept. If progress can be made in this direction, then it may be possible to argue that a certain change does not seriously affect anything central to the institution, for example, but rather affects peripheral and insignificant matters. Clearly, those who differ in their analyses may be led to dispute whether or not a certain change should be regarded as an innovation.

Disagreement about whether or not a certain change has gone far enough may hinge on our calculations of how much the development will in fact alter the educational context, and we may well vary in our estimates of such consequences. And there is an irreducible element of uncertainty here, because the consequences will partly depend upon how seriously teachers respond to the proposed "innovation": persuading them to view it as an innovation may be causally responsible for making it produce more than minimal changes. Thus, "innovation" is sometimes used in an hortative manner. This is particularly the case when the new proposal has yet to be tried and tested.

This dispute also rests at times on differing assessments of how far the schools should go in a certain direction. (There can clearly be disagreements here, even between people who share the view that to do such and such would be to violate the concept altogether.) Hence, if X has in mind an ultimate

The Concept of Innovation in Education / 35

development which is much less radical than Y's, he may well regard a proposal as a good step on the way to his goal, whereas Y views it as a purely token concession or development. A strategy which knocks a second off a mile race is not judged in the same way as one which takes a second off the Boston marathon record. And this is because of different estimates of how far we can go in the two cases.

(b) Secondly, there is the dispute as to whether or not the change is of value, and such a dispute need not involve any of the disputes discussed under a) above, for all parties may agree on the observable facts and concur that the change is "sufficiently different." Other factual issues may arise, however, for X may dispute Y's contention that the proposal will lead to desirable outcomes, e.g., he may believe that the introduction of discussion periods may in fact lead to teachers failing to prepare adequately. On the other hand, he may have objections on *principle* to certain proposals, e.g., to restrict hiring to candidates who are citizens of the country in question. The objections here may range from the charge that the proposal is an outright affront to basic moral and educational principles to the view that it is just not very valuable.

Disagreements then can arise in many ways: 1) people may differ on the *empirical* data; 2) they may not agree on analytic questions; 3) they may fail to reach a common judgment as to whether or not the change is *sufficiently* different because (i) they disagree on how much it will in fact change things, or (ii) they have different ultimate goals; and 4) they place a different *evaluation* on the change because (i) they dispute whether it will produce valuable changes or not, or (ii) they disagree on certain matters of principle. Any disagreement might involve *all* of these aspects or some combination of them. I do not pretend to have compiled an exhaustive list of the sources of dispute in this area, but these seem to be some of the more important. It is not an easy matter, then, to determine what precisely a person is objecting to when he denounces an "innovation." It is surely dubious to draw the generalization that "the climate in support of the innovation ethic is not as hospitable as it might be."[20] Even if every proposed innovation has been rejected, we cannot infer that those who raise objections wish to preserve things as they are, nor that they are opposed to desirable changes. Perhaps they are opposed to any changes whatsoever, but this would have to be established independently.

(iii) On Guiding and Leading

Earlier,[21] I have referred to the *Educational Innovator's Guide*, and to the recent Registry of Innovative Practices in Education, established by the Educational Research Institute of British Columbia. It is crucial to remember that guides, registers, directories, and other lists are compiled for different purposes. One may simply find a list of all the restaurants in town without any comment as to their quality from the telephone directory. A list of the members of a university department does not attempt to say who might be worth talking to or studying with. A guide to the university campus tells you where different groups in the community are located but does not advise where to go. Of course, we can reasonably assume that those listed have met some standard of achievement. The National Medical Register only lists people who are professionally qualified and remain in good standing. Some standard has been attained and maintained by those who are listed. Still, such a book does not go on to say that Dr. X is better than Dr. Y, though some guides do this. Restaurants, hotels, movies may be comparatively rated. We need to ask then: Does the Guide to (or Registry of) Innovative Practices in Education list all practices and proposals which some have claimed to be valuable, or does it merely include those which the authors or directors personally hold to be valuable? If all new proposals are being listed without evaluation, then it is misleading to use the term "innovation." If evaluation has occurred, then the reader should realize that he is viewing a selected list, that it constitutes an assessment which he may choose to reject, and that he is entitled to ask how the evaluation was reached. Before we can intelligently consult a guide, we need to know what task it has tried to fulfill. Sometimes the authors of such guides seem not to be clear on this themselves, for they will claim that 1) their work is based on "valuable suggestions" and 2) that some of the arguments may be "totally indefensible."[22]

Finally, we need to resist the suggestion that educational leadership is to be identified with those who seek innovation.

The Concept of Innovation in Education / 37

This move is fostered by the false view that attention to educational needs necessarily involves making up present *deficiencies*. It has been amply demonstrated that the concept of need also applies to certain things which we *already possess*.[23] Children need to have access to a good library, even if the school has a good library. Educational leadership can equally be displayed by those who seek to preserve what is valuable when it is in danger of being abandoned.

Notes for Chapter Three: pages 132-133

Chapter 4

Calling a Halt: Comments on John Holt's *Escape from Childhood*

It is considered "bad form" by many people to take issue with the claims made by a person who is sincere and only anxious to secure reforms. Really, it ought not to be necessary to point out (though in view of the abuse to which recent empirical researchers have been subjected, it had perhaps better be said) that in assessing the validity of an argument or the conceptual sense of a suggestion, no implication whatever follows about the character of the author. Reference to the author's sincerity is simply irrelevant in these contexts; whether or not a claim is true or false is logically unrelated to the kind of character he has, or his motives in uttering the claim. Sincere people may be misguided, and insincere people may talk sense. The merits of their talk must be assessed independently of any reference to their motives. A similar point has been made by writers in aesthetics who have shown that the value of a work of art is logically unrelated to the intention of the artist.[1] The following comments are concerned with an assessment of certain of Holt's claims, and no inference can be drawn about my view of the character of the person who made them.

My first comment must direct itself to this very distinction, since Holt does not himself observe it. He is attacking "the institution of modern childhood," and his case against this institution is in no way advanced by imputing ulterior and immoral motives to the defenders of that institution. They are alleged to have "this vested interest in the children's incompetence." For the reasons mentioned earlier, this comment is irrelevant. It does, and it logically can do, nothing to weaken the case for the institution. In Chapter 9, Holt notices this himself. He points out, in connection with the sincere but misguided "helper" that "the helping act must be judged by and for itself." This same point applies to the institution of childhood.

Secondly, it is quite commonly alleged to be inappropriate, in some way unspecified, to direct careful analysis towards a book written for a popular audience. The author, I expect to be told, is not a philosopher, and it is "unfair" to employ philosophical arguments against him. It is certainly the case as philosophers have shown, that claims which will not withstand logical scrutiny may be assessed as having value in some other way. Manifestoes, for example, may have great social value even if they contain conceptual oddities. It is, however, worth knowing that a claim is conceptually confused in case we should be inclined to think it literally makes good sense. With this knowledge we are in a better position to know, as we say, how to take the claim—hence, the justification for careful analysis. The fact that the author is not a professional philosopher (or whatever the discipline may be) is once again irrelevant, for one is interested in the claim regardless of the status of its author. Whether or not we are "professionals," the claims we make must logically be of some sort—i.e., philosophical, historical, scientific and so on—and are to be assessed by the criteria and standards which belong to the particular form of knowledge in question. The assumption that Holt's book could not contain philosophically interesting and valuable comments reveals itself at once as an instance of a well-known fallacy (which goes by a variety of names, e.g., the *ad hominem*, or credentialist, or genetic fallacy), in which the truth or value of a claim is assessed in terms of its source. Though the fallacy is well-known, the philosopher cannot tire of his responsibility to remind people of the obvious, for there are clear examples of authors who, in the same article, both accuse others of the fallacy and proceed to commit it themselves.[2] Incidentally, in introducing the logically irrelevant allegation of immoral motives, Holt is himself in danger of being accused of committing this fallacy if, that is, we are being encouraged to reject a proposal or view because X, who defends it, is a wicked person.

Reference to the intended readers of the book has some relevance, for we do not expect to find the same content in an introductory book as in one addressed to advanced scholars. Here the appropriate criterion is "level." False claims, invalid arguments, and conceptual confusion will have no place in an introductory book either. Thus, the second comment on Holt's book must be this. It is quite irrelevant that Holt does not have much faith in arriving at "truth through argument" (p. 5) and that he sees himself rather as offering a "vision." He does in fact employ arguments, and there is no way in which these can be placed above examination. Even if he did not argue, argument might still be deployed against claims which are made. Finally, visions are not always coherent, e.g., a vision of a world full of square triangles.

1. *Judgment*

The central thesis of Holt's book is that the rights, privileges, duties, and responsibilities of adult citizens be made available to any young person, of whatever age, who wants to make use of them. Not all that follows in the book is directly related to this thesis, for Holt often steps aside from his main task to give us his general thoughts on life. Despite his disclaimer, I cannot see that Chapter 6 ("The many 'crises' of life") is relevant to his main topic: that we could learn to do for ourselves much of what we now rely on our doctor to do for us. My only comment here is that Holt relies heavily on the erroneous equation of "feeling fine" and "being well," and this is poor ground on which to build a case against the regular check-up.

Not withstanding the general irrelevance of this example, it will serve well as an example of what we are offered in this book, and it comes to this: the author's intuition. When Holt says "most of what a doctor does," he has not carefully analyzed medical procedures and come to a considered opinion. It is, bluntly, just his guess that we ourselves could do most of this work. And perhaps we could! Guesses are sometimes accurate. But who knows? That is the essence of the problem with the claims in this book. We simply do not know whether to assent to them or not, because the necessary evidence and argumentation is absent. Consider some examples more closely related to childhood: "But I believe that most young people, and at earlier and earlier ages, begin to experience childhood not as a garden but as a prison." No doubt this is very interesting, but how do we know whether or not it is true? Another is "Children want to grow up." This is italicized, but that of course only shows that Holt thinks this is important, or believes it very strongly. It does nothing to show that it is true. In any case, it is necessarily false for the following reason. Some children do not have the concept of "grown up"—a six-month infant, for example. To want X is to have some concept of X. Hence, some children cannot want to be grown up. The claim is not properly qualified, nor is any supporting evidence marshalled. In some cases claims are made for which I am hard put to imagine a suitable empirical test. In Chapter 11, we learn (via the much favored anecdote method) of a young girl whose mother respects her as a person. Holt adds: "Most children are not as fortunate as this one." I, for one, would dearly love to see the empirical test and observations which warrant this staggering claim. Needless to say, none is provided. It is once again just Holt's guess.

Claims of this kind occur in every chapter and virtually on every page. They are the less surprising, however, though nonetheless disquieting, when we read the Preface to the book. We find an anecdote about Martin Buber, the philosopher, in which we learn that Buber declined to advise a man who wondered whether his future son-in-law should become a barrister or a solicitor. Holt quotes from J.H. van den Berg's *The Changing Nature of Man:*

> "Of course, Buber could not know. But nobody asked him to know. What he had been asked for was advice—judgment, not knowledge."

This clearly reveals a totally confused concept of judgment. Judgment is not a guess, or a shot in the dark, but rather a considered opinion based on an examination of the facts and the evidence. "In my judgment" (despite the somewhat debased coinage employed by politicians) does not mean "Off the top of my head, I'd say . . ." To accept the view in the Preface is to believe that, when one reads the unsupported opinion which follows, one is meeting with educational judgments. To follow this path is to abandon a rational approach to educational issues. There are indeed places where Holt openly flirts with this. For example (p. 18), Holt quotes without adverse comment an author whose only judgment on certain traditional child-rearing practices is that "the human race survived them." Even this is tame, however, in comparison with the rejection (p. 22) of scientific inquiry (the principle of causality). This paradigm of rational inquiry, which in fact allowed man to begin to grasp the underlying laws of nature, is reported here as having destroyed much of the meaning of man's world. It is, of course, just silly to pit causality against teleology for, as we have known since at least the fourth century B.C., they provide answers to different questions. We owe this point to the philosopher Aristotle, and it is, I suppose, fittingly ironic that Holt should attribute the destruction of meaning to the "philosophers."

2. Self-Knowledge

One of the chief props of Holt's central thesis is the view that an individual knows better than anyone else what is in his own interests. There can be no doubt that this *is* Holt's view: "But on the whole, most of the time, every human being knows better than anyone else what he needs and wants, what gives him pleasure and joy or causes suffering and pain. Given real choices, people will choose for themselves better than others will choose for them" (p. 115). Philosophical analysis in recent years has shown the mistakes involved in equating the concepts of needs and wants, but Holt runs them together here without any attention to the arguments which have been deployed against this move.[3] A person is no doubt the best judge of what he wants, but the situation is quite different with respect to needs. The concept of need asserts a relation between what is said to be needed and some end-state, and the existence of this alleged relation is to be determined by examining the facts of the case. There is obviously no reason in principle why the individual in question will be the best judge of the facts involved, and it is entirely possible that others will have superior judgment. It is commonly the case that children lack the ability to determine the existence of the relation of need, and hence do not know what they themselves need. Of course, Holt has introduced his view with the vague claims that "on the whole" and "most of the time" the individual knows best. If this is meant to concede that the individual does not necessarily know best, then his view simply reduces to an unsupported empirical generalization. Incidentally, "real choices" implies an understanding of the alternatives, and it is this implication which ensures that young children cannot have certain choices, because they have not developed sufficiently to understand certain ideas.

In one of his earlier books, Holt cites the old saw that if we taught children to speak they would never learn. No doubt there was a point to be made here against some of the inefficient methods we have employed in formal schooling, but nevertheless it is made in a confused way. Children do not learn to speak on their own, and there is clear evidence (derived from gruesome police reports of children who have been isolated from adult contact) that unless language is acquired fairly early in life, it never will be acquired. As Protagoras pointed out long ago, you will not perhaps find professional teachers, but all adults teach children to speak by talking to them and encouraging them to speak. If we waited for children to tell us they wanted to learn to speak, they never would ask this or anything else. Yet, though we do not wait for the child to choose here, because he cannot, we feel quite justified in teaching a child a language. Possession of the most impoverished language is better than none at all.

Holt suggests that the child should make the choice, whatever it is he or she likes best, excepting only such choices as would hurt other people (p. 108). But it is notorious that things we like may do us harm, and may do this without hurting at the time. And there is no reason why a pleasurable experience could not *diminish* our future ability to make reasonable choices, as in cases of drug dependency. Thus, the principle of autonomous decision-making may itself demand much greater restrictions than Holt imagines. And this demand is much more clearly established in the case of persons who do not, or cannot, grasp the dangers in the pleasurable actions they would perform. All children at some stage in their lives necessarily fall into this category. While all children necessarily fall into this group at some time, it seems that all people are in fact liable to fall into it at any time. We could hardly do better than to read Plato's dialogues on this point where the many examples of people erroneously thinking that they know something, surely give the lie to Holt's view that "every human being is likely to know better than anyone else when he has made a mistake" (p. 115). Popular educational theory seems to have forgotten Plato's observation (*Meno* 84C) that a person is unlikely to look for, or attempt to learn, what he thinks he already knows.

In view of his own thesis that people know what is best for themselves, and should only be restricted if their actions are likely to hurt others, by what principle can Holt justify his view (p. 209) that there should be strict requirements for the provision and use of lap and shoulder belts, and stricter penalties for failing to use them? Such equipment serves to protect the occupant of the car, not other road users, and presumably the driver or passengers should be entitled to determine for themselves whether or not they require such protection. If Holt had wanted to protect children as passengers in the car, he could have demanded the right of children to the protection of a seat belt. Even here, on Holt's view, the child would have the right to refuse such protection. In point of fact, Holt has succumbed here to the experts he is fond of denouncing, and is prepared to restrict an individual's freedom for that individual's own good, as determined by an expert on road accidents.[4]

It is, furthermore, curious that while the wearing of seatbelts is to be compulsory, a mere warning is to be affixed to packages of tobacco (p. 194). But leaving this inconsistency aside, how can Holt even justify a warning? In the previous chapter, he had argued for the right "to decide what goes into our minds," (p. 188) and yet he is prepared to insist that the dangers of smoking be brought to the attention of the general public—i.e., put into their minds. The whole idea behind placing a warning on the package is to try to ensure that the user will become informed of something; and in this way his right to control his own learning is violated.

Holt is not merely inconsistent here but also confusing two quite different principles. We surely want people to decide for themselves what they believe, or wish to practise, and this principle is worth defending. But it is not at all the same as deciding what goes into our minds, for not everything which comes into mind is something to be believed or followed. If there were no distinction here, imagination and belief could not be distinguished. The principle defended by Holt has some limited application. Take, for example, a person who may legitimately protest about being constrained even to entertain some notion which he would prefer not to think about at all—an obscene remark, perhaps. But I cannot see that a child has cause to complain that a fundamental

46 / Controversies in Teaching

right has been violated just because he is presented with some ideas by his parents (and not obliged to accept them as true). In any event, Holt's principle could give rise to no possible duty if we are to interact with others at all, for our words and actions will inevitably suggest ideas to other people. Since some ideas are to be suggested necessarily, the real problem (and it is the central problem in education) is to decide *which* ideas to suggest. In this way, value judgments enter into teaching. Far from berating those who think about the consequences of their teaching in terms of the good of the student (p. 188), Holt should applaud those who recognize the serious implications of their interactions with other people.

3. The Right to Learn

It is in this context that Holt asserts the existence of what he terms a much larger and more fundamental right, namely the right to *Learn*, which he is anxious to distinguish from the pseudo-right to be *Educated*. There are, however, good reasons for believing that there is no such general right as the right to learn. Some of these are provided, though not recognized, by Holt himself. To begin with, as Holt recognizes, actions may be restricted if they cause, or may cause, injury to others. But obviously then, some instances of learning activities are to be restricted, for they would involve injury to others. I have no right to learn how much torture you can endure. Holt himself (Chap. 16) brings out the point, by reference to the action which the law will take in connection with a violation of legal rights: that X's possession of a right entails (at least) a duty of noninterference on the part of others. If, therefore, a person had a right to learn it would follow that all others had an obligation not to interfere with that person's learning. But there are cases, (one of which I have cited), where no such obligation exists. The nonexistence of the duty of non-interference in such cases is most clearly seen by the fact that there might well be a positive obligation to interfere, in order to prevent the person from learning something. And this does not only apply to the case in which another person is being harmed, but also to the case in which the person is harming himself or herself. I am confident (Chap. 18, p. 130), that Holt would endorse the following view: all human beings have a right to a secure sense of their own worth.[5] But one might be learning (and let us be clear that this is the appropriate concept) to regard himself or herself as useless. I cannot myself recognize the grounds on which a duty of non-interference could be founded here.

A related right asserted by Holt is what he terms the right of curiosity. Holt seems to believe that if children are taught things which they did not themselves decide to learn, two consequences result: 1) their right to decide what they will be curious about has been removed; and 2) their freedom of thought has been destroyed. This dramatic charge seems to me to be quite false. In the first place, we need to distinguish (a) thinking about issues and (b) looking into issues. Holt runs these together and asserts that adults have the right to decide what they will "look into" (p. 186) and cannot imagine that this right might be taken away. But obviously, while I might be curious about my colleague's salary or private life, I do not have a right to "look into" these matters. Similarly, a child might wonder what will happen if he throws a kitten into the lake, but his right to "look into" this is something else again. Secondly, in being taught something a child is not prevented from being curious about other things; moreover, if he is not taught he may be prevented from being curious about some other things, because knowing nothing of them, or failing to understand, he may not even see the puzzle. I cannot find curious what my colleagues in the mathematics department find curious in tensor calculus, because the problems mean nothing to me. Teaching, then, can open up for an individual new and previously undreamt of curiosities. I have argued elsewhere that there is no *a priori* way of showing that a person could not become educated in the absence of teachers.[6] But there is very compelling empirical evidence that people will not be able to learn certain things without being taught and, left to themselves, may never even stumble on the fact that there is such a subject to be studied. It is not uncommon to find researchers in a given discipline quite unaware that there even exists a body of literature devoted to the philosophy of that discipline. When teaching reveals such new avenues of exploration, the learner's freedom of thought has been enlarged—even though the learner has not chosen to learn. As Holt himself says elsewhere (p. 83), ignorance is not a blessing; it is a misfortune.[7] It is a negative constraint on our freedom of thought.

Holt usefully reminds us of the numerous ways in which our well-intentioned actions may misfire. Experts have taken children out of good homes thinking they might be helping the children (p. 110). And Holt is absolutely right to point out that it is nonsense to tell the state to guarantee what it does not have and cannot provide. He recognizes that "ought" implies "can." But the alternatives are not simply "guaranteed success" or "do nothing." It does not follow from the fact that there are very real dangers in a course of action that nothing useful can be done or that nothing should be attempted. Sometimes risks are worth the taking. There will never be the perfect novel—the idea is senseless— but this does not prevent people, nor should it, from continuing to try to produce better and better novels. Our awareness of the many ways in which teachers have harmed children in the past is not a sufficient basis for the view that the child should decide what, when, where, how, how much, how fast and with what help he wants to learn. There is also the possibility that we might try to eliminate past errors and to find better ways of teaching in the future. It is only if we believe that such improvement is impossible that Holt's suggestion becomes plausible. But what reason do we have to believe this?

4. *Concluding Comment*

I have not appealed to any esoteric philosophical distinctions. My objections to Holt do not rest on complex grounds. A. J. Ayer has commented that "in general, it will be found that the points of logic on which philosophical theories turn are simple. . . . What is difficult is to make the consequences of such truisms palatable, to discover and neutralize the motives which lead to their being denied."[8] I cite this not only because it illustrates a large part of the activity of philosophy of education—namely the application of rules of logic to educational theories—but because it also introduces that sense in which philosophers should be concerned with an author's "motives." (I ignore here disputes about the appropriateness of the word "motive.") What considerations or reasons led him to the view which we want to reject? Can we show persuasively that there is a tempting confusion into which the author has in fact fallen? When I have accused Holt of vagueness, or unsupported claims, or a lack of rigor, or a failure to distinguish similar sounding terms or phrases, it is because these mistakes explain how he is led to educational ideas which will not withstand scrutiny.

Notes for Chapter Four: pages 133-134

Part Two
Aims

Chapter 5

Appreciation as a Goal of Aesthetic Education

It is common to find educational theorists of different persuasions in agreement about certain educational objectives. It would take a rare and brave person to argue that a sense of responsibility was not an objective of moral education, or that critical thinking should be shunned in the teaching of literature. We apparently find it useful to have terms which seem to be virtually synonymous with "an educated outlook" in a particular area. These are labels (pro-labels, of course, for they pick out *desired* objectives) on which we can print our specific educational preferences. Apart from the vaguely desirable aura surrounding them, however, they are empty until the spelling out has been done, and it is at this stage that the disagreement behind the agreement begins to emerge. The utility of the empty label is decidedly limited, and methodological decisions demand much greater clarity about the nature of the objective. Art education reflects the disagreement-in-agreement phenomenon which I have characterized above. The catch-all term which has blossomed into almost universal popularity is "appreciation." It is a term which has recently gained significance in aesthetics generally, having come to signify for many that response which is peculiarly appropriate in aesthetic experience. Such significance, however, makes it more important to be clear on what is packed into the concept if we are to increase our understanding of what constitutes an aesthetic response. Similarly, the increasing use of the term in discussions of art education again argues for careful analysis of the concept, for curricular recommendations will depend to some extent on our understanding of the idea. The purpose of this chapter is not to teach anyone how to use a certain word; the superfluousness of such a task is illustrated by the fact that we know how to use the word already.[1] What I propose to do here is examine the presuppositions, uses, and implications of the concept in order to make it a more serviceable instrument in educational discussions.

1. The Concept of Appreciation

The term "appreciation" is a latecomer to our language generally; the O.E.D. traces it (with one rare exception about 1400) to the seventeenth century. There we find uses which mean "to esteem highly." Several nineteenth-century uses, however, are found which do not contain the idea of a *high* estimate, but more generally the idea of estimating value.[2] Today we are confronted with a wide variety of uses, of which the following are among the more common:

(i) "I appreciate what you did for me," which is one way in which we express gratitude.

(ii) "He threw the girl an appreciative glance," which is one way we can display admiration.

(iii) "I appreciate the point you are making," which indicates that we understand the significance of what is said, and its bearing on the issue.

There has been some temptation in contemporary philosophy to conclude that the different implications contained in the above sentences indicate that the term has different meanings.[3] It can, however, be argued that the meaning remains the same while certain implications vary according to the context. Thus, considering the three uses listed above, it appears that "appreciation" has one and the same meaning in each context, i.e., "to estimate the value of." In the first case, the value of the help given is noted and approved. In the second case, something about the girl (her looks, her comments, etc.) is evaluated positively. In the final case, the worth of a comment in a given context is estimated.

This is not to deny that there are differences, but only to deny that there are different senses of "appreciation." The differences relate to the *kind* of estimation made. For example, I can appreciate a point you are making without being at all grateful to you. You may, after all, be trying to show me up. And I may not admire the point, because I may estimate that it is trivial, generally lacking in significance. Similarly, I can admire your comments without being grateful. If they are not designed to help me, there may be nothing to be grateful for. It is more difficult, however, to separate admiration and understanding, since it is difficult to speak of admiring a point one does not understand.[4] Admiration presupposes understanding. In the same way, gratitude implies praise, and this clearly introduces the aspect of admiration. *A fortiori*, then, gratitude presupposes understanding. In the different uses, we impose a different sort of evaluation, but the estimation of value captures the essential meaning in each case.

The above discussion merely shows that one meaning lies behind several different uses of the term "appreciation" and does not establish that the term is unambiguous. And it may be urged that I have neglected another use of the term in which a different sense of appreciation occurs. Thus the O.E.D. describes one aspect of the concept in terms of being sensitive to delicate impressions or distinctions. This use has been noticed by Harold Osborne,[5] and he claims that the current aesthetic usage is closer to this older meaning. Thus he is involved in two claims, one factual and one conceptual. The factual claim is that contemporary aestheticians do not take as the primary sense of "appreciation" the notion of estimating value. The conceptual claim is that the use of "appreciation" to imply "perception, especially of delicate impressions or distinctions" constitutes a different *meaning* of the term, and that therefore the term is ambiguous.

The factual claim is difficult to assess just because appreciation has only recently gained popularity, and when used is rarely analyzed. One well-known philosophical attempt to offer a preliminary characterization of the concept, however, quite explicitly takes appreciation to mean the estimation of value.[6] And a recent work in art education links appreciation with taste and discrimination, i.e., with judgments of worth.[7] Osborne does not back up his assertion, and at the least my verdict on the factual claim is one of "not proven." More important, I want to suggest that the alleged distinction in meaning is an illusion, and that the one meaning of "appreciation" cited earlier can cover this older usage also. When the term is used to suggest perception or understanding, the idea of the significance or bearing of that which is discriminated is involved. Consider the remark that a person has an appreciation of the fine shades of meaning. This surely suggests that he perceives that there is a significant difference between closely related terms, for example, between conditioning and indoctrination. Appreciating fine shades of meaning involves recognizing that what is said makes a difference, i.e., that it matters, and this is a value judgment.

Consider a case in which questions of significance are removed from the perception. A visitor to an art gallery perceives a delicate impression, namely a fingerprint, which surprisingly countless observers have not detected. It is not the case that such an observation has any bearing on an assessment of the painting; consequently there is not the slightest temptation to speak of appreciation in this context. When a person's comments reveal that he does not appreciate something, it cannot be concluded that he has failed to notice that thing. He can assure us that he has noticed by pointing to the feature, but pointing will not conclusively establish that he appreciates, for this hinges upon the reasons he has to offer.

I suggest, then, that the older use which referred to the perception of delicate impressions can be subsumed under the third group of the common uses cited earlier. Consider one further example, this time from the context of aesthetic education. Suppose that we want to teach a grade X student the concept of dramatic foreshadowing. There may be a stage at which the student understands the phrase, and such understanding could involve distinguishing this from a closely related technique such as irony. Yet the student may have no conception of the use a dramatist can make of the technique; before we are willing to say that the student appreciates the technique, he must have some grasp of the significance or value it can have in a play. This, of course, is very far from being in a position to evaluate the play; it only shows that appreciation of X is the basis for an evaluation of Y, and not, as Osborne wants to argue, that appreciation of X is a basis for the evaluation of X. Certainly the student's evaluation of X may change, increase, and so on, but at the same time his appreciation of X develops.

Osborne cites Munro[8] in support of his own position, but this is questionable. Munro equates appreciation with understanding and enjoyment, and the reference to enjoyment, I suggest, tacitly concedes my point, for it suggests an evaluation. The mistake in this position is to imply that the evaluation is always positive. Appreciation, however, does not rule out dislike, disapproval, and adverse criticism. If we were to read "an appreciation" of a late philosopher's work, doubtless many favorable comments would be found, but fault-finding would not strike us as logically odd. It may seem that a counter to my position here could be urged that on balance there would be a favorable assessment. But even if it is true that such assessments always are positive, this is not a logically necessary truth. Any temptation to think otherwise is explained in the following way. An appreciation is only normally written of a person who is considered by many to have made significant achievements either in a specific area (athletics, science, etc.) or much more generally (moral leadership; e.g., Martin Luther King). However, the particular critic who writes the appreciation may come out against the prevailing view and argue that the person's achievements are grossly overrated. My only point is that, however unusual, this is still an appreciation. Thus, in arguing earlier that "appreciation" has one and the same meaning in all contexts, i.e., the estimation of value, I did not imply that the evaluation is always positive.

2. Appreciation and Enjoyment

Moreover, even if the evaluation were always positive, it would be a mistake to identify appreciation and enjoyment, as B. O. Smith has illustrated.[9] One can appreciate a particular painting, understand what it is trying to say and the point of saying it in that way, recognize that it is a fine example of a particular style or technique, but just not care very much for it. Conversely, of course, a person may derive enjoyment from a painting which he does not properly appreciate.

Admittedly, people sometimes say that they do not appreciate certain kinds of art and mean that they do not enjoy such art. But again, there seem to be contingent factors which explain the rise of such talk, and so the logical distinction remains. It is often extremely difficult to derive enjoyment from a work when we do not understand the significance of it. When we do appreciate, then we are in a better position to enjoy the work; for example, consider the spectator at a game. We do not appreciate and hence cannot enjoy the game. (I am not claiming that this is a logically necessary connection.) Such empirical connections tempt us to talk as if the terms were synonymous. Or again, such talk may indicate a psychological caution. We do not like X, but many other intelligent people do. Perhaps the fault lies in us, and we shift ground and confess that we cannot understand the significance of the work. But our willingness to move to the other expression in the context of a work we do not like creates the impression that the two expressions are interchangeable.

If, however, they were synonymous, what would count as establishing that X enjoys Y would also establish that X appreciates Y,[10] but this is manifestly false. X is the best judge of whether or not he enjoys something, and if he sincerely says that he does, then that establishes the fact. (He may, of course, enjoy the work for what we consider to be inappropriate reasons, but he still enjoys it.) This, however, does not establish that X appreciates Y, for this will be denied if others judge that X provides irrelevant, inappropriate, or generally unacceptable reasons to support his judgment. It makes good sense to say that X does not appreciate *King Lear* if he thinks of it as a comedy.

It is equally important, however, to bear in mind the conceptual connection which holds between appreciation and commitment or caring. If a person does not care for works of art which he claims to value, we are at a loss to understand him. One cannot then appreciate a great work of art and be unmoved at its loss or destruction. Similarly, if I claim that a certain literary form has no aesthetic value (a negative form of appreciation), I must be concerned if my children are spending a great deal of time in its pursuit at the expense of worthwhile literature. For we mean by saying seriously that we value something that we are committed to sustaining, encouraging, pursuing that thing. This logical connection serves further to distinguish appreciation from understanding, perceiving, and noticing.[11] One can notice that something is the case without being in any way committed for or against that thing. It depends ultimately upon what it is that one notices. I can notice something and remain indifferent.

3. Educational Goals

The foregoing conceptual considerations argue for the appropriateness of appreciation as a goal of aesthetic education, but one should notice immediately that the first section shows that "appreciation" does not pick out a response which is peculiarly aesthetic. One can appreciate a philosophical argument without making any judgment of aesthetic worth. "Appreciation" does not refer to some general faculty, for different sorts of estimation are appropriate in different contexts. Quite clearly, a person who is capable of appreciating a complex philosophical problem could be a barbarian in aesthetic matters.

With this disclaimer in mind, however, we can consider the merits of such a description of the objective of aesthetic education. (1) In the first place, it necessarily introduces rational argument and discussion into the educational context, for a person is not said to appreciate unless he is capable of backing up his statements. This is a necessary condition of making an aesthetic judgment at all; that is, we distinguish the "I just like it" response from aesthetic judgment. Thus, if aesthetic education is aimed at developing in part an ability to make aesthetic judgments, it is vital to have reason-giving and justification built into any statement of objectives in this area. I argued in the preceding section that "appreciation" satisfies this condition.

(2) Two significant points relate to my view that "appreciation" means the estimation of value: (i) because appreciation does not necessarily refer to judgments of positive value, this objective does not exclude the study of inferior art works. A powerful case can be made for the view that understanding the fine involves understanding the shoddy. (ii) Since the objective is to estimate value, we do not have to seek further justification for the activity. Extrinsic justifications have proven very tempting in the past; for example, appreciation in order to develop ethical views.[12] But it makes no sense to justify estimating value, for all we can do is to make a further estimate of value. Hence appreciation is pursued for intrinsic interests, and this satisfies a criterion bound up with aesthetic *education*, for education is concerned with the pursuit of intrinsically worthwhile concerns. It is bound up too with the notion of an *aesthetic* judgment, for to view an object aesthetically is to view it for its own sake.

(3) Finally, such an objective satisfies the requirement that the aesthetically educated person does not simply have detached intellectual comprehension but is involved affec-

tively. The concept of appreciation calls attention then to the importance of the education of the emotions in the aesthetic domain.

Notes for Chapter Five: pages 134-135

Chapter 6

Education Amid Cultural Diversity

In recent years the term "culture" has been given a good deal of work to do, and we have heard of the two cultures, the counter-culture, and our cultural heritage. I begin then with an examination of the notion of culture. The term is derived from the Latin word for tilling the land and hence there is a natural connection with cultivation, though there has been a shift from a literal to a metaphorical use. There has been a change of a different nature also in that originally the main application of the term referred to a process, whereas more recently the term chiefly suggests a state or condition. The nominative has gained primacy over the verbal form.

There are, however, a variety of states or conditions which can be suggested by the term "culture," and my purpose in calling attention to these is not to engage in a semantical exercise but to indicate certain significant logical or conceptual points.

1. The Concept of Culture

(a) A Biological Use

This use of the term refers to the development or cultivation of micro-organisms, a procedure of central importance in the diagnosis of certain illnesses. In view of the historical significance of certain slogans in educational theory, it is inadequate to assert boldly that this use is of little educational significance. "Education is growth" it has been said, and hence in the biological use we may have a fundamental model for educational development. I want to argue that such a model is misleading, despite the heuristic value of insisting on the slogan in a situation where education is narrowly conceived as a "stamping in" process. It is not literally true, however, that education is growth, and this is because not all developments count as educational developments. A person may acquire, for example, the character-trait of dishonesty, and this is certainly a development and an instance of learning. But for all that, it is not a case of education. Although we may dispute over specific values (for example, history might be regarded as more valuable than literature) the formal truth remains that we do not regard a process as educational unless (and this is only a necessary and not a sufficient condition) what is being learned is considered to be valuable in some way. By contrast the biological use is value-neutral, for development and growth occurs in the culture, whether it be healthy or cancerous.

(b) A Sociological Use

One way of using the term favored by many sociologists and anthropologists brings us closer to the use which I think is of crucial educational significance, though it resembles the biological use in one important respect. We can call the sum total of ways of living, possessed and transmitted by any society, a culture. This sociological use does not commit the speaker to approving the customs and behavior patterns which he observes, and thus, it resembles the biological use in being value-neutral. A sociologist can, without linguistic impropriety, speak of the culture of Nazi Germany, though he may abhor many of the practices which he describes. This use, however, is also importantly different because it brings the term into the human realm. In this sense, only human beings have cultures; and the plural is not insignificant, for a culture is something which belongs to a set of human beings. Robinson Crusoe had a distinct pattern of existence but it would be odd to speak of his culture in this sense. It is shared public conventions, customs, ways, mores, habits, practices, traditions, concerns, and pursuits which constitute culture from the sociological point of view.

This value-neutrality is admirable in the context of sociology, for the discipline of sociology is empirical and, like physics, not concerned with value questions. It is, of course, interested in describing value systems but not in assessing them.

(c) A "Committed" Use

Once we speak of a person as cultured, or of the place of culture in the life of a nation, it is clear that we have abandoned neutrality. Culture in this sense is not just development but improvement of the mind. Often it is more narrowly conceived as mental improvement in a certain area, notably "the arts." This is the sense of culture referred to by Matthew Arnold when he spoke of the best which has been said and thought in the world. If the things about which someone is knowledgeable, or in which he is interested, do not fall into the category which we regard as "the best," we will not refer to that person as cultured. Others, however, who reject our valuations, might be willing to say that he is cultured. I regard this use of the term as being crucial in educational theory because education too is concerned not simply with achieving mastery in some sphere, but mastery in an area which is considered valuable or worthwhile.

(d) A Culturally Diverse Country

It seems to me that this description of a country could operate at two levels. On the one hand, it might simply imply that in a given country one could reasonably claim that there are two or more distinct patterns of life. Doubtless there would be complex interrelationships between them, but for all that they would be distinct. In this case, the term "culturally diverse" would be operating on the sociological model. It should be clear that a cultural distinction of this sort is not something which is "obvious," or a "plain fact"; it is, on the contrary, a highly complex and sophisticated interpretation. On the other hand, "culturally diverse" could indicate that in a given country different groups disagreed in their evaluation of certain pursuits. This sort of disagreement might take the form of a clash between traditional and more recent forms of art—for example classical versus popular music. It might be thought that these two levels collapse into one. If on the former model we find one group following one pattern and a second group a distinct pattern, does this not indicate a clash in evaluation of a style of life? I do not think this obliterates the distinction. We might find distinct patterns in one country without rival evaluations, for a group may pursue one style of life because of custom and tradition. It clearly does not imply that they have considered and rejected other styles of life. Yet in the disputes over the merits of forms of art, preferences do often represent a conscious and rational decision, a fully fledged evaluation. Such rival evaluations need not entail the existence of two or more distinct patterns of life.

2. Educational Implications

(1) We may begin by considering the case in which cultural diversity implies a prevailing clash over standards and evaluations. I am not thinking of the kind of disagreement which exists when one school of literary criticism rates a particular dramatist more highly than another. The classical dramatists each have their devotees. But at this level, the disputants are willing to concede that the other dramatists are worth reading, and rightfully claim the attention of the cultured person. Shakespeare may be supreme but life is long enough to enjoy Marlowe also. A clash of a different order exists when "beat poetry" is said not to be poetry at all, "pop music" is not serious, or a piece of fiction is an entertainment but not a novel. Here, poetry, music, and the novel have standards of evaluation built in, and other variations are said to fall short of the standard. Yet serious voices can be heard on the other side, calling attention to valuable aspects of the new culture.

It is not difficult to think of the name of the intellectual skill required in this kind of context, that is, discrimination. Difficulty arises when we ask what is packed into this term. Let me make the following points:

(a) Discrimination implies conscious, rational choices, based on a grasp of the problem. It is contrasted, for example, with guessing, or just opting for something.

(b) Discrimination comes into situations in which a solution, decision, or choice cannot be determined by the application of a convenient rule.

Teaching, then, in this area cannot always involve giving the student the answer: he is, to a great extent, on his own. But the teacher can provide him with a grasp of the problem at hand and can always at least put him into a position to show discrimination. I particularly like the word "encouragement" in this context, for teaching, which takes different forms depending upon what is being taught, involves recognizing discrimination in embryonic form and stimulating its development. We need not conclude that the existence of such a value dispute implies that the teacher must remain neutral, or attempt to avoid the issue. His responsibility is to examine representative forms of culture critically and rationally. This point will be considered further in Chapter Eleven.

(2) Cultural diversity, as we have seen, can also imply that there exist side by side two or more distinct patterns of life. Since this use of culture is value-neutral, I must begin by making the following point. If, as I argued earlier, such a sociological use allows us to speak of Nazi culture, for example, it follows that the process of education may involve shaking off one's own culture. Many will find this latter idea unacceptable, even abhorrent; but this seems to me to depend upon a confusion of the sociological with the "committed" use. Clearly, with the latter use in mind, it does seem paradoxical to speak of education involving the elimination of one's culture. It is, however, part of the concept of education that it refers to something valuable. Hence if aspects of one's culture are worthless, immoral, or unjust, acquisition of those behavioral patterns cannot count as becoming educated. It will not do in the sociological sense of culture, to define the purpose that education ought to have as developing a commitment to one's own culture.

A further preliminary question requires consideration. Which other cultures, i.e., patterns of life, are Canadian students to examine, from among the world's countless possibilities? A selection must be made, but what principle of selection should be employed? I think a rational case can be made for giving priority to those other cultures which most directly impinge upon one's own. I do not mean here to offer a utilitarian defence of what our schools should concern themselves with. However, if education is centrally concerned with the development of understanding, then it is reasonable to take into consideration the *problems* and *issues* which will call for understanding in the student's life. Certain topics and pursuits will throw more light on the student's pattern of life than others, because he will not be able to understand his own unless he understands the relationship with another. An example here would be the necessity of studying some English history in the context of Canadian history. Thus, I believe a case can be made for giving a measure of priority to the various cultures within a country on educational grounds. I stress this because these sorts of considerations, rather than political ones for example, are relevant in determining a school curriculum.

(3) The first consideration of the educator in this context is with the provision of information and knowledge on which further intellectual and moral responses can be based. (The word "provision" here is meant to be neutral with respect to matters of methodology.) I suggest then that curriculum planning in the area of cultural diversity should consider as a prime objective (a) the development of awareness of the fact of cultural diversity. It follows from the points I made earlier that (i) all aspects of the curriculum will be affected, since "culture" in this sense refers to a whole pattern of life. Clearly, history, social studies, literature, music, physical education, and so on can indicate the existence of cultural diversity. It might be thought that science would constitute an exception here, since the procedures of science are not culture-bound. On the other hand, the value which one culture places on science can differ from that of another, and moreover some cultures have tests of truth which are considered superior to scientific tests of truth. How far these remarks are true of cultures within Canada is a matter on which I am not competent to speak. I only wish to make the general point that science too can provide illustrations of cultural diversity.

It follows that (ii) such an awareness does not imply at this stage distinctions which relate to merit or worth. Indeed such distinctions of relative merit depend upon a sound awareness of the substance of various cultures. Awareness of the fact of cultural diversity is logically independent of judgments of value. The development of such awareness is surely the first step in the elimination of "cultural blindness" which infects many school systems.[1]

This first objective cannot, of course, be achieved in the abstract, for students learn such an awareness by focusing on examples of diversity. But this can be done without going far into the nature of the cultures referred to by way of example. Such in-depth probing constitutes the second goal of educators in this area which I characterize as (b) the development of an understanding of other cultures. I hope it is clear that this objective is distinct from the first discussed. The dif-

Education Amid Cultural Diversity / 67

ference is essentially this: knowledge that X exists does not imply understanding what the nature of X is. This point is confusing because ordinary language sometimes allows "know" and "understand" to be used interchangeably. For example, if asked "Do you know what I mean?" a person can reply "Yes, I understand," and this is perfectly acceptable. On the other hand, we can also recognize the following kind of statement: "I know what he is saying, but I don't understand him. I can't see what he is getting at." It is possible to know many things about another culture without really seeing what they add up to. For example, an Indian tribe abandons its aged to certain death in the wilderness. It takes a good deal of familiarity with the thoughts, feelings, and concerns of these people before we can say what this practice reveals of them and their character.

It is perhaps worth indicating certain common sources of misunderstanding in order that teachers can guard against them:

(1) *Isolationism.* This is the error of taking a practice out of context, of failing to see how it relates to a broad pattern of life. The intellectual skill required here (and once more Matthew Arnold can help us) is the ability "to see things steadily and see them whole."

(2) *Translation.* By this label I do not mean to suggest merely a *linguistic* problem, although this is one example. Rather, I suggest the mistake of reading what we see in terms of our own cultural pattern, our own conceptual framework. Landes has the excellent example of the refusal by children of certain Plains Indian tribes to answer questions in class. This all too readily translates into "failure" in our conceptual framework, but actually represented a refusal to engage in boastful practices.[2] Clearly the errors of isolationism and translation often go together.

I do not wish to underestimate the seriousness of the linguistic barrier. Our language enshrines all the distinctions which our cultural tradition has felt worth making, and our words are infused with subtle overtones, allusions, associations, and emotions. Another language may not have the distinction we have drawn, or may have drawn it in a different way. These considerations make linguistic translation an extremely complex and intellectually demanding exercise, and also serves to indicate an ever present source of confusion.

(3) *Lack of Imagination.* Some of our customs and habits are so much a part of our way of life that it is hard to conceive of another group of people not having them. A child may be understandably bewildered when he hears that another culture does not have the idea of apologizing in its conceptual framework. It is not that everyone is rude, but that they do not have the concept of an apology. Again, when confronted with a practice which we find abhorrent, for example, killing a child born with some deformity, there is a possibility that we will raise a barrier again. Imagination is, of course, not something in which students can be drilled, rehearsed, and trained: rather it is to be cultivated and encouraged. My guess would be that poetry and novels are crucial in its development.

These, I suggest, are some of the *main* difficulties which stand in the way of the development of understanding, though I do not pretend to have given an exhaustive analysis. It is important to realize that understanding does not imply agreement or support. Some expressions in ordinary language are potentially misleading in this respect. For example, we hear people say "I just cannot understand how he could assault a baby in that way." The feeling seems to be that if we say we understand, we bring the action into the sphere of acceptable human actions. We want to call attention in a dramatic way to our horror and we do so by regarding the action as incomprehensible as a possible human action. Clearly, however, psychology and sociology can go a long way to explain such actions, and we can to that extent understand them. But, for all that, our moral condemnation remains firm. Coming to understand customs and practices in other cultures, then, does not mean that students are coming to approve of them. Even the expression "an understanding person" which does imply concern and sympathy, does not mean that the person approves of the matter in question. "An understanding" is an agreement, but this may only be an agreement to differ.

While the development of understanding does not imply that the student comes to approve, neither does it ensure that he necessarily develops sympathy. Intellectual development does not guarantee moral development. It seems to me that education in this context should be concerned to encourage the emergence of a certain moral attitude: more specifically, a third goal of education in the context of cultural diversity is (c) the development of respect for persons.[3] This attitude essentially involves recognizing that others also possess fundamental human rights. The principle is violated when, for example, we show contempt for issues and customs which others value greatly. People can, of course, lose our respect in various ways. They may display character-traits of which we disapprove, such as dishonesty. But when in such a case a person loses our respect, it does not follow that we have violated the principle of respect for persons. We do not admire them, but yet we accord them the rights and privileges which go with being a human being.

It is of course, possible to admire a person even though we disapprove of his actions. It is my view that the genuine conscientious objector is in this category. This observation is crucial in the area of cultural diversity, because it is surely the case that often those practices which we condemn in another culture are followed conscientiously. Suppose, for example, that a particular society defends the practice of torturing political prisoners. We can condemn the practice without necessarily holding those who conscientiously follow this practice *blameworthy*. Moral education must make clear the following possibilities:

(1) We can condemn a person and his views without violating the principle of respect for persons.

(2) We can admire a person without supporting his views.

Recognition of these points imposes restraints upon the person who wishes to act from the moral point of view. I have been arguing then that the educated person shows respect for the beliefs and customs of others in the sense that he recognizes that they are the beliefs and customs of other human beings and this recognition imposes restraints upon the ways in which he can condemn such beliefs and customs should he wish to do so. If the customs and beliefs are condemned in legitimate ways, those who uphold them may yet deserve our admiration.

70 / Controversies in Teaching

This discussion reinforces the point made in the earlier analysis that questions of evaluation are centrally involved in educational matters. Questions of condemnation arise because the process of education seeks to determine which customs, practices, and beliefs are worth preserving. If "education" encapsulates a standard of value, we cannot define education in terms of coming to accept one's own culture, because there is always the possibility that elements in one's own culture are worthless. Education, then, must involve submitting the practices and customs within one's own culture to rational assessment. It follows that a fourth goal of education is (d) the development of critical ability.[4] An indoctrinated person is unable to consider objections to his own beliefs in a rational and detached manner. Since the state of being indoctrinated is incompatible with that of being educated, it is clear that a necessary condition of being educated is open-mindedness, an ability and indeed willingness to consider objections to one's own beliefs.[5] The existence of cultural diversity, and an educational program which encourages the development of awareness and understanding of other cultures, makes it imperative to devote serious attention to the goal of encouraging critical ability. The fact of cultural diversity necessarily means that students will be encountering beliefs and customs which differ from their own. This particular aim of education is disturbing to many people, and not surprisingly, because it seems to me to be a conceptual truth that one's own culture will involve beliefs and customs we cherish. And we are not willing to abandon them lightly. Of course, the development of critical ability may serve to increase our appreciation and admiration of our own culture. Despite the threat to beliefs which we cherish, as educators it seems we have no alternative but to subscribe to this goal, unless arbitrary restraints are to be imposed and open and rational discussion in our classrooms sacrificed. When education seeks to develop critical ability it is clear that we are closer to appreciating culture in the sense which refers to the best which has been said and thought in the world.

Notes for Chapter Six: page 135

Chapter 7

Education and Cultural Disadvantage

In the wealth of material which has appeared in recent years on the educational issues associated with cultural disadvantage, precious little has been contributed from philosophy, concerned with an analysis of the crucial concepts involved. Indeed it is a pardonable exaggeration to say that problems associated with cultural disadvantage are regarded as falling within the realm of empirical inquiry, more specifically within the social sciences.[1] It is, for example, the sociologists who have attempted to identify and characterize those who are culturally disadvantaged. No part of my task here is to challenge the *accuracy* of their research findings, but an appreciation of the significance and relevance of them depends upon clarity at the conceptual level. Although the sociologist often heads the inquiry with a question such as "What is it to be culturally disadvantaged?" which calls for a conceptual inquiry, this invariably (and understandably, given the purpose of the discipline) is treated as the question "What are the features, traits, circumstances and attitudes of those who are disadvantaged?" And this latter inquiry clearly *presupposes* an understanding of the concept. We find an interesting and useful catalogue of factors contingently related to disadvantage but no explicit examination of criteria which are logically related.

1. The Logic of "Advantage"

An examination of the concept shows that the orientation described above is seriously misleading. One implication of speaking of an advantage is that one person has something someone else does not have, or is in a position to obtain it more readily than that other person. But examples clearly show that this condition is insufficient. If X has pneumonia and Y does not, it is not X but Y who is better off. Or suppose that X has a choice between taking the bus or the subway to work, whereas Y can only take the bus. If, however, this is a perfectly adequate means of transport in Y's circumstances, he is not at a disadvantage. Even in a case where X values what he has, Y may not be at a disadvantage because he does not have it. For example, X has the chance to marry a certain young lady, and Y does not, but Y is not the least inclined towards her. On the other hand, Y may not on occasion realize that something he is unable to obtain, for example an education, is valuable, and we may say that he is disadvantaged though he does not realize this and hence does not recognize grounds for complaint. Similarly X (a boxer) may have an advantage over his opponent and not realize this. On other occasions when an advantage has to be *seized*, recognition is vital.

Three important points emerge from these cases. In the first place, discussions about advantage are not purely empirical or factual and therefore claims made in these matters are not purely social *science*. Fundamental evaluations are involved in saying that X has an advantage. This latter claim would not be allowed by those who believe that what X has is of no value. Secondly, the people who are said to be advantaged or disadvantaged are not necessarily the best judges of their own circumstances. Hence the disadvantaged are not to be identified with those who actually raise complaints. The logic of "disadvantage" is such that it is not determined by what Y *does value*, but by what is regarded as *of value*. Thirdly, the ascription of these labels is essentially a comparative activity. X may be advantaged in relation to Y even though X's own situation fails to meet a minimally acceptable level for human beings. For example, X has something to eat while Y is starving, but X is eating garbage. This does not conflict with the previous claim concerning evaluation for although we would not choose to eat garbage were other foodstuffs available, it is *better* than starving to death. This comparative aspect is one way in which "advantage" differs from "opportunity," for it makes *sense* at least to speak of everyone enjoying the same opportunity, whereas "equality of advantage" would be an absurd principle. Moreover, one can always ask "In what way?" when someone is said to be disadvantaged and the adjective supplied picks out the form which the person's disadvantage takes.

It is worth noting that every advantage does not constitute a case of injustice. Advantages may be deserved and undeserved. Karpov may have an advantage over Korchnoi when the latter loses his queen, but the cry of injustice cannot be raised if Karpov has worked for and earned this advantage. But because an advantage may be unfair, it is not at all odd on occasion for someone *not* to want a favorable position with respect to the acquisition of something of value, which he also values. Ordinary language is potentially misleading in connection with this general point, because there are certain idioms which do imply an injustice. When we say, for example, that X *took* advantage of Y (the latter's innocence, ignorance, credulity, helplessness) we do imply that X has acted unfairly and is blameworthy. But this is clearly *idiomatic*. We can also say that X took advantage of the situation and praise his resourcefulness and imagination. This point does mean that a good deal of the emotive force and rhetoric of recent writings evaporates. "Disadvantaged" has been used as an effective slogan, but the serious planning of educational objectives and strategies demands more careful attention to the assumptions involved in its use.

2. *Educational Issues*

Certain forms of disadvantage do not pose problems which relate to the central purposes of educational institutions. If Y is disadvantaged in that he has access to less milk than his school friends the result may well be that this disadvantage will hinder his school work. My point is that when schools get involved in the distribution of free milk, this activity is not itself an *educational* one. The school is here engaged in other highly desirable forms of activity, in this case serving as a social welfare agency. Our first question then concerns the nature of the activity when the school seeks to remedy *cultural* disadvantage. The term "culture" refers to a shared pattern of human life, including customs, conventions, habits, mores, practices and traditions. To refer to such a pattern of life as a culture is *not* to indicate approval or disapproval. By contrast there is a more limited use of the adjective "cultured" which refers to an *improvement* of the mind, generally restricted to "the arts".[2]

It seems clear that, as it is used, "culturally disadvantaged" does *not* pick out just one form of disadvantage. The following are among the more important uses:

(a) X belongs to a culture which is disadvantaged economically, socially and other ways;

(b) X belongs to a culture but is disadvantaged because he has to operate within some other culture;

(c) X is disadvantaged because he belongs to an inferior culture when he might belong to another;

(d) X is disadvantaged because he cannot appreciate certain aspects of his own culture.

This list makes no pretensions to comprehensiveness.

Let me illustrate the ways in which the three conceptual points made earlier bear upon some of these uses. First to *the value criterion*. In the prevailing skepticism over value judgments, it is not surprising that we encounter such a statement as the following from Kenneth Johnson:

> "Furthermore, it is not possible to place a value on
> any culture and label one better than another."[3]

In this particular case it is wise to follow Hume in thinking it best to leave an antagonist of this kind to himself in the likelihood that he will "from mere weariness come over to the side of common sense and reason".[4] A few pages on, Johnson admits:

> "Still there is some truth in the implication that the
> experiences of disadvantaged children are different
> in quality."[5]

Without some value judgment, the concept of disadvantage would simply idle. In (d) above, for example, the experience of some people *within* one culture are judged to be inferior in quality to those of some others. Remedial work here might well entail educational activities, for X may not appreciate certain aspects of his culture because he cannot understand what they involve. Similarly in (c) X's disadvantage may be that he is growing up in a culture which seeks to indoctrinate him with an ideology which holds that a certain group of people are less than human. Here again there is room for legitimate educational work, for such claims are open to rational and critical scrutiny. Implicit here, of course, is the position that education cannot be identified with the process of initiation into one's own culture, for major elements of this culture may be worthless.[6] In (b), which is one of the more common uses of the phrase, the value criterion is again clear, for it is only when it becomes *important* or *necessary* that X live within some new culture that he becomes disadvantaged. This is brought out by the conditional statement "X would be disadvantaged if he had to . . ." which is used in such cases. Again, there are educational processes related to the alleviation of such disadvantage. Much of X's disadvantage will stem from prejudice and lack of certain basic skills. Concerning prejudice (which X may find in the members of the new culture or which he may bring with him) I do not want to make the naïve claim that schooling *will* be effective in changing attitudes, but rather the logical claim that the prejudiced outlook is at odds with the outlook of an educated person. The latter involves making rational judgments on the basis of available evidence, and precisely this is absent in the former. Secondly X's lack of certain skills, for example vocational, social, linguistic, may be made up through the processes of education. The crucial question which remains when it is determined that through learning X can come to operate within a particular culture, concerns the worthwhileness of what is to be learned. Unless it can be shown that the practices are valuable, they could not be taken as educational objectives. The scholars who could not or would not participate in Nazi culture were not disadvantaged in any sense which called for their further *education* in *that* culture. When they moved away from Nazi Germany, they were of course often in need of further education.

In some cases, for example (a) above, many of the disadvantages call for fundamental social reforms and government intervention rather than new educational programs. Of course, education has a contribution to make in that it may influence the climate of opinion out of which wide-ranging programs of reform may emerge.

The second point relates to the claim that *others may be in a better position to understand* someone else's disadvantage. For example, if X grows up as a member of a minority culture surrounded by prejudice and a feeling of hopelessness, it may not be possible for him to develop what Rawls has characterized as "a secure sense of his own worth."[7] Here X does not consider *himself* as having value. This is the *nature* of his disadvantage that he fails through no fault of his own to recognize what is of value. It is others who must plan the experiences which can help X to achieve that sense of his own worth which is a basic human right. Curricula, therefore, cannot simply be based on the felt wants and demands of the disadvantaged for the latter are not always able to appreciate the nature of their disadvantage.

Finally, we may comment on the *comparative* criterion. Since, as we argued earlier, one person is disadvantaged in relation to some other, it will not do to assert that the disadvantaged still enjoy a level of educational opportunities beyond some minimally acceptable level, if our concern is for a *just* educational system. It may be that a minority culture in the United States is less advantaged than a white middle class group, but nevertheless better off than even an advantaged group in some other society. Such a claim is sometimes made concerning the non-white groups in South Africa. But even if this claim were true, it would not alter the point that there remains a deep and objectionable injustice unless it can be shown that such disadvantages are deserved.

Notes for Chapter Seven: pages 135-136

Part Three
Teacher Education

Chapter 8

Teaching: Preparation and Certification

1. The Traditional View Under Attack

There is a long and respected tradition of thought which holds that the selection of a teacher is an issue of the greatest seriousness. Socrates reported that he had said to Callias, who had spent a great deal of money sending his sons to the Sophists for their education:

> ". . . if your sons were foals or calves, there would be no difficulty in finding someone to put over them; we should hire a trainer of horses, or a farmer probably, who would improve and perfect them in their own proper virtue or excellence; but as they are human beings, whom are you thinking of placing over them?"[1]

Nor was this a chance remark. The importance of careful and informed choice of one's teachers is discussed at length by Socrates in the early part of the *Protagoras*, and provides the rationale for the subsequent examination of the sophist.[2]

The point is not, of course, that the historical commentators on education have agreed on the substantive issue of what constitutes the necessary and desirable qualities of a good teacher. Not everyone would agree with Rousseau, for example, that being a foreigner, or a priest, should *disqualify* a person from teaching in public schools.[3] The agreement concerns the more formal point that attention to the qualifications of the would-be teacher is requisite. There is room for disagreement on the question of what those qualifications should be.

The traditional view then rests on the assumption that there are certain standards which a teacher should meet and it urges that parents or the state should diligently investigate the credentials of those who wish to teach. This latter is typically stated in language which suggests that it is a very serious moral responsibility. What I have called "traditional" would probably be called downright old-fashioned by many for whom that is *not* the name of a virtue. All this worry is misplaced for since we all have potential as teachers, we can safely leave teachers to select themselves. John Holt has recently suggested for example that people might volunteer to act as "reading guides":

> "What about testing the guides? No need for it. There is no reason why a guide should be able to read or write every word he might be asked."[4]

More recently, Herbert Kohl has devoted the first chapter of a book on reading to the question "Who is qualified to teach?[5] It begins:

> "Anyone who reads with a certain degree of competency can help others who read less well. This is the case regardless of age or previous educational training."[6]

It goes on:

> "Teaching need not be the province of a special group of people nor need it be looked upon as a technical skill . . . If you have a certain skill you should be able to share it with someone. You do not have to get certified to convey what you know to someone else or to help them in their attempt to teach themselves."[7]

Before coming to an evaluation of these contemporary views, it is important to clear away certain red herrings which only manage to muddy the water.

There is in the first place the strong *suggestio falsi* that if only we had not been corrupted by the powerful doctrine of competition which prevents us from sharing our knowledge with others, we would readily assent to the view that we all have potential as teachers.[8] These questions are, however, logically distinct. We may, for example, regard competition as often undesirable and sharing knowledge as presumptively good, and still maintain, on other grounds, that certification and attention to qualifications is important. This tactic is, however, a useful ploy in debate. It is a species of that common genus "Confuse your opponent as to the issue at hand."

Secondly, we must notice the deliberate attempt to discredit the traditional view by imputing ulterior and outrageous motives to those who defend that position:

> "Of course professionals, in order to maintain their special claim to teaching or law or medicine, encourage our feelings of inadequacy and incompetence."[9]

My objection here does not relate to the truth of this controversial claim, nor even to the fact that in introducing a controversial claim Kohl blandly asserts "of course"; it is rather the logical point that such an observation is quite irrelevant to the question of the merits of the traditional view. Even if every defender of that view has acted out of personal and selfish considerations, the truth or falsity of the view is to be assessed independently of these matters. My motive in praising your work may be to obtain a favor. But your work may well be praiseworthy, and my acting from this motive does nothing to show that it is not praiseworthy.

2. A Crucial Ambiguity

Kohl writes that "you do not have to get certified to convey what you know" and we can, of course, assent to this. It is *not* a logically necessary condition of conveying knowledge that a person has been specially authorized to do so. But in assenting to this, we should notice that we are not thereby committed to any particular position on the *different* question of whether or not it might be *desirable* to have a system of public scrutiny of credentials in the case of teaching.

"If you have a certain skill you should be able to share it with someone." Part, at least, of Socrates' concern would be made clear, if we were to add some qualification such as "provided that the skill is not itself evil, e.g., the art of torture, and that it does not prevent a person from acquiring more desirable skills." This is one legitimate reason for an examination of those who propose to teach, similar in kind to the justification for the exclusion of quacks from medicine. Socrates, indeed, wished to claim that the grounds of justification are strongest in connection with education because "you cannot buy the wares of knowledge and carry them away in another vessel; when you have paid for them you must receive them into the soul and go your way, either greatly harmed or greatly benefited."[10] I think this stronger claim is both unnecessary and incorrect. It is not necessary because we only need to show that good grounds can be adduced for assessing those who propose to teach, and not that these grounds are more important in this case than in some, or any, other case. But the argument is invalid because it fails to distinguish 1) the case in which the student understands a pernicious doctrine *and* is corrupted by it, from 2) the case in which he understands but is not harmed. Socrates seems to suggest that "receiving into the soul" will be *necessarily* harmful or beneficial, and this is false.

In short, then, we need to add *ceteris paribus* to "if you have a certain skill you should be able to share it with someone." A person should not, other things being equal, be prevented from sharing what he knows with others, and we would need to include here a reference to internal constraints, i.e., he should not acquire the constraining belief that competition always outweighs sharing, or the belief that sharing always demands prior, and special, authorization. Indeed we might go further and regard sharing a skill as not only morally permissible but, on occasion, morally obligatory.

None of this, however, helps to support the case against preparation and certification. Indeed the necessary addition of the *ceteris paribus* qualification points up the need for public scrutiny. Furthermore, the moral injunction, like any other, presupposes that the person *can* do the action in question. That we advocate sharing where *possible*, in no way establishes that it is possible in any particular case. It is the "can" claim which is here in doubt. But the sentence which I have analyzed here as a *moral* comment is susceptible to another interpretation which hinges on an ambiguity in the words "should be able." "A man should be able to vote freely" is very probably the assertion of a moral right. "We should be able to get the refrigerator through the door" is clearly not. This statement asserts our belief that it will probably be *possible* to do it. It is vital to keep these two senses apart in thinking about the statement "if you have a certain skill you should be able to share it with someone." Taken as a moral claim, it is, suitably qualified, acceptable. But taken as the view that if X has a certain skill it will probably be *possible* for him to share it with others, it becomes a very dubious empirical claim. We can say two things confidently: 1) it is not *necessarily* the case that a good practitioner of a certain skill will be good at getting others to share it. No contradiction follows from the denial of the alleged connection between possession of a skill and ability to share it (and this has nothing to do with the person's willingness). 2) We know *in fact* that many people who are experts in a certain skill are not at all good at initiating others into that skill. We have no general grounds then for claiming that the expert *will probably be able* ("should be able" sense 2) to initiate others. If the acceptability in principle of the moral claim—sense 1—tempts us to slide into accepting sense 2, then quite obviously teacher preparation will appear otiose. Sense 2 suggests that the expert or the possessor of a skill is necessarily, or at least very probably, able to teach it. But there are no good grounds for believing that this is true. The acceptance of sense 2 *would* remove the need for professional training—save as a means perhaps of polishing up an ability one already possesses—and would make *teacher* certification pointless. It is worth noting, however, that it would not destroy the need for *certification* itself. The sentence closely analyzed is, after all, hypothetical and we may properly ask: Does X possess the skill? The Socratic objection to exposing our children to charlatans will apply here also. If *per impossibile* to possess a skill were necessarily to be able to teach it, we could still legitimately demand that X's possession of the skill be attested to by certification.

3. The Case for Preparation and Certification

Plainly it will not do to protest that it is obvious whether a person possesses a skill or not. There are just too many examples of people who have managed to disguise their incompetence, sometimes for years. This fact does *nothing* to show the pointlessness of teacher certification *in principle*, though it does, of course, reveal that such practices are not always very successful. It is extraordinary, however, that when the appropriate step to take is to *improve* a practice, it is commonly suggested that the practice be *abandoned* altogether. We cannot do it perfectly, so let's not do it at all!

Even if we could eliminate the rogues from teaching, and assume universal sincerity, this would not do the trick, for people may sincerely believe that they possess a skill when they do not. Protagoras boldly, and perhaps sincerely, said:

> "Young man, if you associate with me, on the very first day you will return home a better man than you came, and better on the second day than the first, and better every day than you were on the day before."[11]

—but there is some doubt about the very existence of such a skill, let alone whether or not Protagoras possessed it. Holt's self-appointed reading guide may sincerely think he knows when he does not, and as a result may *misguide*. The metaphor of "teacher as guide" which strongly appeals to Holt and Kohl is really deceptive here. We are led to believe that professional training and certification are associated with some limited, and objectionable, form of teaching such as "forcing information."[12] We condemn this practice *and* everything associated with it. Then we turn to "guiding and assisting" with which we feel much more comfortable, and hey presto! training and certification have disappeared. The sleight of hand is helped by the fact that guiding and assisting are, of course, nontechnical words which have a regular use in ordinary, unspecialized, non-professional contexts. But in any context, if some things will count as guiding and assisting, others must necessarily count as leading astray and hindering. And we are entitled to ask whether a prospective teacher is likely to do the former or the latter. This, I assume, allows in the question of a person's qualifications. And even if no special training is necessary for *some* cases of guiding, this does nothing to establish the controversial claim that training is never necessary for any case of guiding.

These objections are in no way undermined by the fact that Kohl's views appear in a book about reading. Firstly, his opposition to training and certification are stated in quite

Teaching: Preparation and Certification / 85

general terms and not expressly limited to the teaching of reading. Secondly, the objections hold in the case of the teaching of reading also. It is true, of course, that a five year old may be able to teach someone else to read. But the concept of reading includes,[13] as Kohl recognizes,[14] such matters as the critical interpretation of difficult works and not every reader could teach reading here.[15]

There are, of course, objections which can legitimately be raised against the use of the concept of *training* to characterize the kind of preparation required by a teacher, but these objections do not show that no form of preparation is needed, hence they do not support Kohl's position. It might be argued, for example, that the notion of training does not do justice to the open-ended nature of the teaching situation in which the teacher may have to abandon a generally useful rule or technique.[16] Or again, that training fails to make a necessary connection with the development of understanding, and is compatible with mere know-how.[17] It is for such reasons that I deliberately employ the general and neutral term "preparation" in my title. Debate over the appropriate characterization of teacher preparation is quite distinct from debate over the question of its necessity.

I have tried to show then 1) that the case for public scrutiny of credentials (certification) would not be destroyed even if professional training were not necessary, for we would still want to determine whether or not a person did possess a skill, and what kind of skill it was. And 2) that we have been given no good grounds for believing that some form of preparation is not necessary. This second point can, however, be buttressed by some more positive observations. Firstly, teaching involves the selection and implementing of various tactics or strategies in order to promote learning.[18] It is, then, possible that a person could make inappropriate selections and/or ineffective efforts at implementation. Secondly, even if one could naturally, and without special preparation, make some progress, there is the possibility that preparation could enhance one's achievements. These points simply indicate that empirical research in psychology, sociology or methodology may reveal that certain intuitively attractive strategies do not work, or serve only too well to promote an undesirable outcome; and that even the naturally gifted may become better.

It would be reassuring, rather than embarrassing, to learn that these points are obvious. It only becomes necessary to reiterate them when they are so commonly neglected or even denied. It is significant, however, to notice that even those who acknowledge the need for teacher preparation are willing to make certain important exceptions. There is, of course, nothing wrong with this, provided that the exceptions are based on relevant distinctions. The most important single exception is, I think, the case of university teaching. There is in Canada, for example, no practice, and scarcely any talk of developing a practice, of programs in teacher education for those who intend to teach at the university level.

I do not think that the resolution of this question hinges on the conceptual and normative problems relating to the purposes of the university.[19] If it is held that there is a place in the university for a person who devotes all of his energies to research, questions of teaching ability are not relevant. I am, of course, referring only to those who intend to *teach* in the university. Nor will it do to argue that the university does not properly concern itself with teaching, that this is merely incidental to the real purpose of the disinterested pursuit of truth. For if even this were the case, the very fact that the university *does* engage in teaching makes it entirely reasonable that students should be taught by the best available teachers.[20] Teaching may not be central to the university's task, but this in no way removes the harm which may be done by exposure to incompetent teachers.

Are there any particular differences in the university context which could defeat the general presumption in favor of preparation and certification established earlier? Reference is sometimes made to the *vulnerability* of the learner at the early stages of education as one such difference.[21] There may well be differences of degree here, but university students remain vulnerable. There are a number of dangers: 1) they may fail to develop an interest in a subject which might have had intrinsic value for them, 2) they may come to misunderstand the nature of a subject, 3) they may be subjected to quite irrelevant propaganda and indoctrination. Is it plausible to maintain that university students are necessarily able to offset these dangers? Or truthful to maintain that such things never occur in universities? I think not. It is clear how courses in psychology and methodology might help to offset the first and second types of danger. What is not clear is how preparation or certification could help to prevent the third. Quite obviously, a prospective university teacher may successfully conceal his ultimate propagandist intentions. Here, however, public scrutiny has to be understood as an on-going examination of a teacher—the continuing informal assessment by colleagues in the community of scholars. If there are any absolute goods, tenure certainly is not one of them, for a clear case of systematic and deliberate indoctrination would constitute reasonable grounds for dismissal of a tenured professor. And this simply because indoctrination can have no place in a university.

Let us not despise, however, those rare moments when some *practical* value may be claimed for philosophical studies. A conceptual inquiry into indoctrination, education, open-mindedness, bias, and related notions in a teacher education program may help the prospective teacher to avoid those actions which will only serve to develop an indoctrinated outlook in his students. The one who wants to educate may unwittingly work against himself, and one source of this is an inability to clearly characterize one's goals.

Notes for Chapter Eight: pages 136-137

Chapter 9

Models of Field Experience

Whenever a term or an expression which has served well for a considerable period of time begins to give ground to another which covers much the same kind of activity or object, it is well to ask what change, if any, we are making in our conceptual ordering of the world. There will be, clearly, many possibilities. The old term may have taken on new and unwelcome connotations. The new term may call attention to important changes in the activity; or possibly, the activity has remained much the same, but the way in which we conceive of the activity has altered. A case in point is the declining popularity of the expression "practice teaching" which served to mark out that period of time which a student teacher spent in a school teaching under supervision. It still occurs of course,[1] but increasingly is being replaced by other expressions including the one I propose to examine later in this chapter, namely Field Experience. There are, I think, two general defects with the term "practice teaching". First, it seems to suggest that learning to be a teacher simply involves rehearsing or practising certain methods which the student-teacher has learned *about* in theory. "Practice" is at home with those activities in which we can be *drilled;* that is, activities which are comparatively limited in scope and which have a restricted range. Learning to be a teacher, by contrast, involves the acquisition of discrimination and judgment, qualities which are open-ended in the sense that they are not covered by a set of rules.[2] The teacher must not only be skilled in certain methods, he must know when to use a particular method; i.e., he needs a sense of judgment, and this is not covered by a skill-oriented term such as "practice." Secondly, the term "practice teaching" did not call attention to other valuable aspects of a period spent in a school by a student-teacher. It is a time, for example, to observe, to discuss, and to discover one's reactions to the future role. It is for this reason, that many writers feel that "practice teaching" refers to just one aspect out of many, and that "practice teaching" should be seen as one part of Field Experience. This is valuable, but it does not avoid the defect pointed out in my first comment on the term above.

Sometimes the word "practice" is opposed to "real." For example, "We're not really playing, just practising." But, of course, when the student teacher teaches it is teaching in a literal sense, although I am aware that there are elements in the total situation which we might want to call "unreal"; e.g., being constantly under supervision. Still it is really teaching, just as a practice match is still a football game. For this reason, I believe that "teaching practice" was a better form of expression, for this at least clearly implied that it *was* teaching.

I do not want to suggest that the expression "practice" is entirely without merit. Insofar as the term "practice" implied that, as in the musical arts, skill, expertise, and success demanded patient effort and hard work, the term had its good points. For teaching, like playing the piano, is something that the teacher has to work at if he is to succeed. Yet, just as "practice," which is quite at home with the beginning student at piano, becomes more and more inappropriate as we approach the accomplished pianist (though the latter must keep playing!) so too does the term fail to do justice to the activity of teaching.

What has happened is that we have become clearer about the implications of "practice," and evolved a wide concept of teaching and recognized that the two are not well suited. The term has not taken on new connotations, but changes have taken place in our concept of teaching, and also in the ways in which we conceive of the purposes of spending a period of time in a school. I want to bring out some of these conceptual changes, and I propose to do this by examining the notion of Field Experience. This has a vaguely appealing ring to it, partly I suspect, due to the widespread view that "experience" of any sort is valuable.[3] The general agreement that the expression refers to something valuable, however, conceals hidden disagreements about what is valuable in Field Experience and why. This is not a term which has a simple meaning, nor one which bears its meaning on its face. The different interpretations can be discussed in terms of different models and it is to these that I now turn.

1. The Apprentice Model

The term "apprentice" is at home in the area of trades and crafts. Initiation into a particular trade has typically been by way of a system of apprenticeship; that is, placing a young person in the care of a skilled person in that area for a specified time. This conception of teacher education does justice, it must be admitted, to Aristotle's remark that the things a person has to learn to do before he can do them, he can learn by doing them. The application of the model in its essential form is witnessed in the monitorial system used in England and the United States in the nineteenth century.

In apprenticeship systems emphasis is laid on "knowhow" rather than on theoretical understanding, although I do not wish to imply that the former cannot generate the latter. The apprentice is being trained, and training can certainly lead to intelligent and skilful practice, yet it is logically compatible with an absence of a grasp of underlying principles. Apprenticeship concentrates on a fairly restricted field, i.e., a particular craft, and does not seek to develop an understanding of the relationship which a particular craft may have with another. I find that these implications are unsatisfactory in the context of teacher education, hence I regard the change in terminology from teacher training to teacher education as a conceptual clarification. First, teacher education must be concerned with the development of an understanding of underlying principles. Given that not everything which can be taught is educationally desirable, reasonable decisions about what to teach need to be made. Such decisions presuppose familiarity with general principles. Secondly, the teacher cannot be confined to a narrow area, whether this be a specialty such as history or a level such as elementary, and remain ignorant of the relationship which exists between his work and that of other teachers. If he is to be effective in developing one form of knowledge, such as history, he will need to have some understanding of the relationship between this and other forms of knowledge, such as science and mathematics.

In a recent defence of training, B. O. Smith has asserted that training does not cripple innovative capacity. This is correct, of course, but does not affect the above criticisms of the training/apprenticeship model. The point is that training does not say anything about the need for innovation, for a grasp of principles and for cognitive perspective. Smith writes,

> "A trained individual has relaxed control which frees him from preoccupation with immediate sets so he can scan the new situation and respond to it constructively."[4]

We can recognize the truth here if we think, for example, of driving a car in modern traffic conditions. It is important that the skills become second nature so that we can think about complex situations as they arise. The point remains, however, that the apprentice model does not stress the importance of the latter reference to critical rational judgment. The best that can be said for it is that it is not a model which actually rules out understanding as a conditioning model would.

The 1971 report on teacher education in Prince Edward Island[5] rejects the craft-concept of teacher education but the reasons appear to be that this concept denies the usefulness of teacher training, and thus represents unwarranted pessimism; and the concept fails to distinguish between knowing something and knowing how to teach it. But to the first of these, a defender of the model would clearly say that the only disagreement was about the form the training would take. The defender of the apprentice model is not committed, as the report suggests, to the belief that teachers are born, not made. It could be argued that the teacher is "made" during the period of the apprenticeship. Hence, it is important to show, as I indicated earlier, fundamental difficulties in the view that a teacher could be produced in this way. I fail to see that the second objection is apposite because typically in an apprenticeship a person is learning how to do something. It is true, of course, that knowledge of X does not imply ability to teach X, but the defender of the apprentice model is concerned with the development of skill in teaching. My objection here is the different point that "knowing how to teach" cannot simply be regarded as a skill, but calls for judgment and understanding.

2. The Anthropologist Model

An assumption built into the apprentice model of Field Experience is that a student is necessarily a teacher in preparation, that is, a person who is learning how to be a teacher *in order to teach*. If we conceive of the student teacher as an anthropologist, no such assumption is made. On this model, Field Experience gives a person the opportunity to enter the schools, to make empirical observations about the nature of schools and assess the value of the experiences which the pupils are being given. The uppermost consideration of the student teacher is to *understand* the practices, mores, customs, conventions, and attitudes that he or she finds displayed. The assessment should, of course, be as objective as possible, based on careful examination of evidence, as befits a scientific study. The student should enter the school with an open mind, prepared to abandon his preconceptions if there is evidence against them.

There is much in this model to commend it to student teachers. It calls attention to the fact that cultural and linguistic differences will create communication problems and the student teacher is liable to misinterpret what he sees because he reads the evidence in terms of his own framework. Thus, this model emphasizes the necessity of understanding and critical reflection on experiences which the previous model glosses over. The model brings out the point that there may well be many practices in contemporary education which the student will want to reject. The Field Experience should not be seen as a chance to familiarize oneself with current practices in order to accept them and learn to operate within them. This virtue of the model could only be denied, it seems, by claiming that there are no defects in contemporary practice, or that, if there are any such defects, the student teacher has no right to criticize them. I cannot believe that anyone would make the former claim, but the second one sometimes enjoys a hearing. Now even if it were agreed that a teacher has no right to criticize the school system, this model is anxious to emphasize that the student teacher is not yet committed to a school or to this career, and surely no one will deny that the student has the right to choose not to enter this role.

There are, nonetheless, certain deficiencies in this model. For one thing, student teachers have typically lived in the kind of society, i.e., a school, which they are now to examine, and this is not typically the case as the anthropologist approaches a society. Secondly, it is a fact that most student teachers *are* preparing to join this particular society, to enter a role in the school community, and this again is atypical of the anthropologist. The model then suggests a false degree of detachment. I certainly agree that a student should approach the system in an open-minded way, and that he retains the right to reject the role if he finds it undesirable in some way. However, students are, in the main, concerned also with learning how to operate in a particular role in the school community, and not simply understanding what the role entails. Of course, it might be said that the fact that most students are preparing to enter this role is regrettable, since the system as such is indefensible,[6] hence the model has the additional merit of detachment. The anti-school position is one which must be met at the level of rational criticism and not simply rejected. But the anthropologist model will not further the debate at a rational level because it begs the question against the system. Since it is a fact that the typical anthropologist is not preparing to commit himself to the society he studies, the model would introduce this as the norm for student teachers. It would, as a result, be "unusual" for a student teacher to enter the role. The student who decides to commit himself to the role of teacher in a school community cannot regard Field Experience as an anthropological exercise. Moreover, the student teacher has a decision to make for or against the system, and this decision is not required of the anthropologist and hence not suggested by the model. Anthropology is an empirical discipline concerned to describe and to explain rather than to evaluate. But the student teacher must make an assessment, and a model of Field Experience should suggest this.

3. The Intern Model

This term has recently come into favor in Canada, notably at Simon Fraser and McGill Universities, and was endorsed by the Committee on Teacher Education at the University of Prince Edward Island. This report declares that

Models of Field Experience / 95

the term "implies a long period of practice after completion of formal studies." The writers compare this period with the medical student's internship and the lawyer's period of articles. There is no doubt that the report seeks to create a more favorable image of teacher education and this serves to account for the analogies drawn with the medical and legal professions. For example, in rejecting the apprentice model the Committee comments that "no one would apply the craft concept to other professionals such as doctors, dentists, engineers, and architects." The report speaks of "internship" as a new *concept*, but I fail to see that length of time sufficiently distinguishes internship from practice teaching. The latter expression says nothing about the length of time required. As a matter of fact, the period of internship is normally longer than the period formally spent in practice teaching and this is no doubt desirable, but it hardly generates a new *model*.

More significant, I believe, is the point that internship presupposes a period of formal studies. This does distinguish internship from the apprentice model, for the latter ignores the importance of theoretical understanding. I use the word "presupposes" advisedly because the Committee, rightly, I believe, does not hold that formal courses must precede practical experience. Indeed they suggest that practical experience precede studies in educational foundations. The important point is that the model does stress the value of theoretical understanding, and it remains a practical problem to decide upon the most advantageous ordering of the experiences.

Internship is a wider notion than practice teaching, for the intern is not only concerned with developing certain teaching skills; in addition, he observes other teachers, establishes relationships with students, and in general concerns himself with the enterprise of teaching rather than simply with the activity.[7] "Practice teaching" as a concept seemed to suggest more narrowly a concern with the activity, probably because of the close association between practice and skill learning.

Thus far, surely, the model is an improvement because a student teacher is hoping to develop his knowledge and understanding of the enterprise of teaching in general. But the dictionary reminds us that the verb "to intern" means "to confine within prescribed limits," and these are surely undesirable associations. In the first place, we do not have definite prescribed limits in teaching: there is a good deal of disagreement about aims and methods, though we do seem to be reaching agreement about certain undersirable aspects of teaching. Even if we were to reach general agreement, however, there is not likely to be a very narrow set of limits and there will always be room for innovation and criticism. One of the observations made early in the Prince Edward Island report—that the tasks performed by such professionals as doctors and dentists are more clearly definable and that their procedures are more securely developed—is, I believe, a consideration which tells against the importation of the concept of internship into teaching circles. It is perhaps for these reasons that the medical profession does not reject the associations of the term "intern." There is wide agreement in medicine concerning the aims of the profession, and disputes normally concern techniques and methods. Issues relating to value judgments, however, continually occur in education, for the concept implies that worthwhile activities are being pursued. Hence a model of Field Experience is inappropriate to the extent that it neglects the need for personal value judgment.

I think it is clear that the three models which we have seen above have features which commend them to our attention. The apprentice model reflects the truth that teaching ability is something which needs to be learned and developed. But it ignores the point that experiences are not self-explanatory and require interpretation in the light of concepts and theories, a point which the intern model emphasizes. This model in turn, however, tends to assume that the theoretical underpinning is fairly clearly mapped out already, and in this way puts a halter on the student's own judgment. It is on just this point that the strength of the anthropology model appears, for detachment and independence are the marks of the disinterested scientific approach. The difficulty here is that an emphasis on cognitive assessment of this kind ignores the notion of initiation which can be an aspect of Field Experience and a point which the other models bring out. Hence, my conclusion, which should not be surprising, is that we cannot reasonably follow one model to the exclusion of the others if we are to understand the nature of Field Experience. As Scheffler has remarked in another context,

> "Like all models, they simplify, but such simplification is a legitimate way of highlighting what are thought to be important features of the subject."[8]

Field Experience relates, as I have shown, to a complex series of activities, experiences, and circumstances and a simplifying model can only draw attention to certain aspects at the expense of others.

Notes for Chapter Nine: page 137

Chapter 10
Philosophy as a Vocational Handicap

Try to imagine a person who has spent four years at an institution of higher learning engaged in the following practices: questioning the assumptions of modern science; examining the forms of valid argument; probing fundamental moral issues; studying views and claims advanced in the area of aesthetics; wondering about the status of religious beliefs; considering the general theories about life and nature which have been developed in the history of thought; and pondering the very nature of knowledge itself.

It would not be at all strange to learn that such a background had provoked an interest in educational theory. Imagine further, then, that such a person devotes a year to the study of educational thought, to the philosophy, history, psychology and sociology of education. During this time attention is given to various methodological matters and an opportunity is found to gain some practical experience of teaching.

This brief thought-experiment concludes with the following challenge. Try to imagine the look on this person's face when he or she discovers that the local school system has no place for a person so prepared. That is, it is apparently believed by those who are responsible for hiring teachers for the schools, that such a background does not constitute a preparation which would justify selecting this person to contribute to the educational development of children. It is not simply that there may be other, more valuable backgrounds, but that this particular background does not even advance the person to *candidate-status*. This person is not *considered*.

Though our imagination has been sorely tried in the foregoing, I have not in fact recounted a fable. My three opening paragraphs merely describe 1) the good honours graduate in philosophy, 2) a year of scholarly and professional work in education, and 3) the present licensing regulations in the province of Nova Scotia.[1] Some readers may remember the somewhat humorous evaluation sheet on Socrates which circulated a few years ago, in which low marks were assigned for 'heavy Greek accent' and the like. In Nova Scotia this is no joke—under present regulations, a latter day Socrates *could not* be hired.

1. An Ambivalent Attitude Towards Philosophy

As curious as this may be, further investigation unearths the Alice in Wonderland effect. Not only is the honours graduate in philosophy excluded, *no* applicant for a teaching position may even cite a philosophy course as a relevant aspect of his academic preparation. A teacher, for example, will be required to have a certain number of courses in mathematics if he is to be licensed to teach mathematics, but he may not count philosophy of mathematics as one of these. I have even heard of a case in which *one and the same* university course, which is offered under two descriptions, is acceptable under one, and inadmissible under the other which describes it as 'philosophy of.' Such a case might tempt one to interpret the situation as involving a mere prejudice against philosophy, but such a line of thought comes unstuck in the following way. Whereas courses in philosophy such as philosophy of science or philosophy of mathematics are not to be regarded as part of a student's scientific or mathematical education, philosophy of education invariably appears as a required course in a B.Ed. program. Without such a course, the student cannot gain a licence.

I believe that the ambivalence reflected here rests in part on an ambiguity in the term 'philosophy' bolstered by certain historical practices. 'Philosophy,' and hence the phrase 'philosophy of education,' can mean different things in English. One distinction is particularly relevant here: (i) there is an unrestricted use of the term 'philosophy' as in such comments as 'my general philosophy on this is . . .' or 'my philosophy of education rules out the use of punishment.' This use suggests something like a person's general or overall view on something, and clearly a person's general views might be based on economic, psychological, historical, religious and other grounds. One of these grounds might also be (ii) the discipline of philosophy as practised in university—the careful examination of arguments and concepts and the examination of forms of justification. For example, a philosopher asks: 'What do you mean?' (e.g., by number) or 'How do you know?' (e.g., that the child *understands*, i.e., what are the criteria of understanding?) Philosophy of X then, asks such questions about X, whether X be education, art, mathematics or whatever.

Philosophy in sense (ii) is relevant, indeed necessary to arriving at one's philosophy sense (i) but it is not *sufficient*. It is not sufficient because other sorts of considerations are necessary if we are to arrive at adequate general views about, say, the teaching of mathematics. For example, for sense (i), one would need knowledge derived from empirical psychology about how *in fact* children acquire the concept of number and such a question cannot be answered by armchair-tied philosophy sense (ii). But the same example illustrates the *necessity* of philosophy sense (ii) because unless the empirical psychologist has done some conceptual work on number, how could he conduct his research? Put bluntly, he would not know what he was looking for!

Now it may be that the apparent ambivalence is explained in the following way. In connection with 'philosophy of education,' education authorities have in mind sense (i)—i.e. a teacher should spend some time thinking about his general views about education. Historically, courses given under the title 'Philosophy of Education' have often ranged beyond philosophy sense (ii) to include theories of child development, social theories, school law and myriad other things. Very often too, philosophy sense (ii) has been completely ignored! Modern philosophy of education courses which interpret philosophy of education as a branch of the discipline of philosophy only began to emerge about twenty-five years ago. By contrast, there has been no tradition interpreting philosophy of science in sense (i).

Thus, the situation is merely a paradox, an apparent contradiction. Philosophy is valued by educational authorities when taken in one sense and not valued (or not valued very much) when taken in another sense. If it is true that educational authorities do not appreciate the significance of philosophy sense (ii) in a teacher's general education, this seems to me to be most regrettable. That such a view should rest on the notion that a course is irrelevant because that course *itself* will not be taught by the teacher is absurd. Many other subjects which a teacher does not actively teach may obviously illuminate the subject which he does offer. A high school teacher of mathematics may not teach 'The Philosophy of Mathematics' (though I see no reason in principle why this would not be a very suitable option in the upper grades) but that does not imply that his teaching of arithmetic and algebra may not benefit from his own knowledge of the philosophy of mathematics.

2. Two Probable Objections

Two further arguments, however, may be expected against the inclusion of philosophy of X in the education of a teacher of X. (a) Granted that the philosophy of X has intrinsic merit and interest, in the crowded timetable of a student teacher there is just not time and we must concentrate on teaching courses within the student's area of specialization, and (b) many eminent mathematicians and good teachers of the subject had no special knowledge of philosophy of mathematics.

Let us begin with (b). I would want to distinguish quite carefully between the roles of researcher and teacher in any given area. It is quite possible to do good work in a discipline without being able to talk much sense about that discipline. But the *teacher* is concerned to explain to others unfamiliar with a discipline what that discipline involves, what is distinctive about it and how it compares and contrasts with other disciplines. All these activities involve reflecting on the *nature* of his subject, i.e., *philosophical* reflection. Of course, a teacher can do much good work without being able to do these things, hence the counter-example in argument (b); but there will be an important side to the activity of mathematics teaching which will be outside his or her scope. The mathematics educator does not merely wish to teach others how to 'do' mathematics, but to convey an understanding of what mathematics is. He can hardly do this if he does not possess such understanding himself.

Coming to argument (a), we need to beware of a piece of sophistry. Arguments which assert that there 'isn't time' masquerade as comfortable factual claims, when in reality they are dubious value judgments.[2] It is only the case that there 'isn't time' for philosophy of mathematics in the education of a teacher if there are other subjects which we believe to be *more worthy* of study and these exhaust the time available—and how much is that anyway? If it is really important, time must be found, perhaps by extending the period of teacher preparation. Of course, it would be foolish to suggest spending time on *philosophy* of mathematics at the expense of work in mathematics. Work in philosophy of X in any case presupposes knowledge of the activity X whatever it may be. A person with no mathematical background cannot get far with philosophy of mathematics.

It seems to me that perhaps in the philosophy of education course, a student teacher in the area of mathematics might be encouraged to sample the literature on the philosophy of his subject. The teacher of philosophy of education will probably not be able to talk usefully about all the various philosophies which relate to the school curriculum, but students in various subject areas could be guided towards the literature in their own area. Scheffler has recently reported that many students are quite amazed to find that such literature exists![3] This is not to condemn the various specialist departments in the university, for it is only reasonable that they would see their central task as teaching courses in the discipline. On the other hand, it might be stimulating if various members of a department got together occasionally to reflect on the nature of their own discipline. For those students who take a special interest, a specialized course in philosophy of mathematics, for example, (normally to be found in the Philosophy Department) might be appropriate.

3. Philosophy in the Schools

The general point made concerning (a) above also has relevance to the question of the study of philosophy in schools. It is not at all clear to me on what grounds the subject of philosophy is excluded from the *Program of Studies in the Schools of Nova Scotia.*[4] Not only is the view that there 'isn't time' for philosophy inherently controversial for the reason given earlier, the Nova Scotia Department of Education *cannot* take this view if their own statement of aims is seriously intended. The statement stresses the importance, among other things of discriminating among values, acquiring an analytical attitude towards change, critically examining the exercise of authority and influence in society, freedom of thought and inquiry, an appreciation of the aesthetic aspect of life and the development of a better understanding of oneself. The latter echo of the inscription at the Delphic Oracle cannot but put us in mind again of Socrates, for, having been pronounced the wisest man in Greece by the oracle, he came to the realization that this consisted in an awareness of the fact of his own ignorance. It was indeed in the writings of Plato that the elimination of 'the vain conceit of wisdom' is first assigned a central role in the activity of philosophy. It was with respect to his failure to observe the injunction to 'know thyself,' that the sophist is essentially distinguished from the philosopher. The aims listed, far from ruling out philosophy, require that philosophy be *ruled in*, for they logically cannot be approximated without philosophical reflection. That is, it cannot be asserted without absurdity that philosophy is not relevant to the objectives cited. Of course, philosophy may not be as useful as some other activities, such as typing, with respect to some other aims mentioned in the *Program* such as being able to earn a living. But I assume that a subject is not to be discounted because it fares badly with respect to *one* objective since I cannot immediately see how mathematics (which *is* a subject in the *Program*) is conducive to sound physical health (which is also one objective). In any case, it is not at all clear that it is desirable to plan a curriculum on a purely utilitarian or vocational basis. Philosophy may be a vocational handicap, but on this basis we are not entitled to infer that it lacks intrinsic worth and interest.

There are, however, other considerations which, if applicable, would justify the exclusion of philosophy. There are, for example, some fairly obvious reasons why low temperature physics is not introduced in Grade 1. For a long time, even those who recognized the value of philosophy thought that it could not be profitably studied by students of school age. There is now, however, a rapidly growing body of evidence which indicates that this assumption is unfounded, and that valuable work in philosophy can be done even in the early grades.[5] Even if philosophy is not introduced as a distinct subject into the schools of Nova Scotia, it is surely indispensable that philosophy *pervade* the curriculum in the sense that each teacher brings the philosophical and critical spirit to bear on his or her particular area of interest. If the Provincial Department is to encourage this, and to pay more than lip-service to its stated aims, the value of philosophy in a teacher's preparation must be explicitly recognized.

Notes for Chapter Ten: pages 137-138

Part Four
The Role of the Teacher

Chapter 11
Controversial Issues and the Teacher

In the area of controversial issues, there are certain normative and methodological questions of concern to the teacher. The former category includes those problems connected with the school's responsibility and with the teacher's rights. For example, is the teacher entitled to outline his personal views on the issue? The questions raised in the latter category depend upon the normative position taken earlier. Thus, the methodological question might be: how does a teacher maintain a neutral position? In this paper, I begin with a question which is logically prior to normative questions. This concerns the problem of an adequate *analysis* of the nature of a controversial issue. Possibly this exploration will cast light on the subsequent questions.

1. The Nature of Controversy
The importance of beginning with the analytic question is perceived by Stenhouse in a recent and stimulating paper,[1] but there are certain errors in the analysis he offers. Stenhouse quotes with approval a definition offered by Dorothy Fraser:

"A controversial issue involves a problem about which different individuals and groups urge conflicting courses of action."[2]

But it is not the case that all controversial issues are such that the recommendation of a *course of action* is involved at all. Consider, for example, the contemporary controversy in medical research about the effectiveness of vitamin C in inhibiting the onset of the common cold.[3] In such cases, as in all scientific and empirical controversies what is primarily at stake is *what is to be believed.* Stenhouse misses this, I believe, because as his title suggests he is primarily concerned with controversy over value questions. It is vital, however, not to offer an analysis of the nature of controversial issues which blurs the differences between value disputes and scientific ones.

Further comments quoted from Fraser and added by Stenhouse also fail to apply to controversial issues in general. Thus, Fraser is quoted as maintaining:

> "It is an issue of sufficient significance that each of the proposed ways of dealing with it is objectionable to some section of the citizenry and arouses protest."[4]

And Stenhouse offers his own summary:

> "In short, a controversial issue is one which divides teachers, pupils and parents."[5]

The previous counter-example shows clearly that these generalizations do not apply to all controversial issues. Pauling's claims with regard to vitamin C do not arouse protest among the citizenry. Many controversies pursued in learned journals are of no concern to the citizenry. Nor are teachers, pupils and parents necessarily divided, for, without the necessary background in the particular discipline, a person cannot even understand the issue. It scarcely makes sense to speak of taking a side on an issue one does not understand.

Thus far I have argued that Stenhouse's analysis will not apply to all controversial issues. I want to suggest further that certain of his claims do not even apply to controversial *value* issues. He claims that:

> "It is specific cases which make for controversy; there can be no interpretation of practical values in the adult world which does not deal with specific cases. Thus, that war is an undesirable thing is scarcely controversial, but whether the war in Vietnam is justified is highly controversial."[6]

There are, however, sizeable groups in Canada, for example, who condemn abortion, divorce and birth-control in quite general terms. Stenhouse has been misled by the examples he uses and overlooked controversial value issues which do not relate to specific cases.

We can approach a more adequate analysis by recalling a comparison used earlier linking controversy and dispute. A controversy is necessarily a dispute, but the converse does not hold. Thus, if a husband and wife have a dispute about some domestic issue, we would not refer to this as a controversy. The reason is, I believe, that the dispute is essentially private. Yet earlier I criticized Fraser and Stenhouse for making reference to the citizenry. The problem here was that certain controversial matters do not involve the general public. Rather, I suggest that a controversy is a dispute in the public forum, the latter phrase being relative to the issue in question. Thus, Pauling's claims are controversial because, although the general public is not involved, the relevant public, i.e., the scientific community, is involved. Furthermore, the dispute must not be *settleable* by readily available procedures, though we may know how to go about resolving the dispute. In this way, not every disagreement in the public forum amounts to a controversy, for some can be terminated at once, for example by checking the relevant documents. Such a solution does not obtain in the case of Pauling's views, for while we know what would *count* as conclusive evidence for or against the theory, the construction of such an experiment is complex, and a resolution of the issue cannot readily be determined.

Not every dispute, of course, reaches the relevant public forum. We need here to attend to what *counts* as getting the issue into this arena. It cannot simply be, for example, that a dispute is made known to the members of the relevant community because geographers and others are *aware* of the claims made by the Flat Earth Society. This issue, however, would not be described as controversial because such claims are not taken *seriously*. When we describe an empirical dispute as controversial we, who are perhaps on one side, do at least take the other view as a plausible alternative. We may feel quite certain that it is mistaken, but there is enough of a *prima facie* case to treat it with respect. This, I would say, accurately describes the position that Pauling's views are in today. His own eminence, coupled with the research he has conducted (admittedly limited), demands that he be listened to, however erroneous his views are thought to be by the vast majority of researchers. Had I, for example, made the claims which Pauling has made, the issue would almost certainly not have become controversial. I would not have been able to *disturb* the consciences of the scientific community.[7]

It is important to notice that value questions can reach the public forum (often, but not necessarily, the general public; for example, controversies in the realm of aesthetics) in a different way. This difference hinges upon the way in which we are disturbed. In the scientific case, it is a matter of being aroused from our "dogmatic slumber" by a good opposing case. The value issue of apartheid is controversial, however, not because we believe that a case has been made against our conviction that racial groups should be treated equally, but because we regard the consequences of the system to be so pernicious that we must be concerned. Again, we are disturbed when others refuse to allow their children blood transfusions, not because we believe that there is even the slightest justification for such a belief, but because the rights of others are threatened by such a belief.

Thus, it is only sometimes the case that a controversial value issue implies that each side has a certain respect for the views of the other. For example, the work of James Joyce led to vigorous controversy concerning the literary merits of his novels. As in the scientific case, the opponents could take each other *seriously,* and moreover the dispute could not be readily settled. What was required in this case was sustained literary criticism, a weighing and re-evaluation of the works—a process which has resulted in a decisive triumph for Joyce's admirers. But the kind of mutual respect present in this case, is not necessarily present in a controversial value issue, nor is it necessarily implied by the description "controversial." To summarize, therefore, in describing an issue as controversial we mean:

(1) that it is a dispute of some significance in a public forum;

(2) that the resolution is not readily available;

(3) that it is disturbing, though the factor which disturbs varies from case to case.

The second condition might be objected to on the grounds that certain controversial issues can be readily resolved. In the area of proposals and recommendations, a political nominee may be a controversial choice. But this controversy will evaporate if the candidate steps down. Similarly in a value dispute, one side may simply withdraw its controversial claims. It will be noted that such withdrawal is not possible in the area of a controversial empirical dispute. No one would be satisfied if Pauling simply ceased to press his case. Here I am not just making a psychological point, but more significantly an analytic claim. His claims only become controversial when a sufficient *prima facie* case is established, and it is an analytical truth that such a case is not answered by ignoring it, or failing to press it. One cannot logically just *abandon* a *prima facie* scientific case as one can a proposal or value stance. It is doubtful, however, that such abandonment in the latter case can be identified with a ready settlement. When the controversial nominee steps down, the controversy may die away, but the issue has not been settled as it has, for example, in the case of Joyce's work. Rather, one side chooses not to press for a settlement but gives up the contest. I am not claiming that all settlements must represent a *compromise*, for in all kinds of controversial issues a complete conversion is logically possible and would constitute a settlement. It must be remembered, however, that we only begin to call proposals and value judgments controversial when people take them seriously enough to make issues of them in the public forum, and such conviction makes a ready settlement normally unavailable. I suggest then that the three conditions are separately necessary and jointly sufficient for an issue to be controversial.

Traditionally, the normative issues alluded to in the opening paragraph have covered two major problems: first, should controversial issues be *included* in the curriculum? The second question, which arises if and when they are included, concerns the rights and responsibilities of the teacher in the *handling* of them. I believe that the foregoing analysis can contribute to a consideration of these problems.

2. The Inclusion of Controversial Issues

I wish to discount all arguments in favor of including such issues which make use of extrinsic considerations such as preparing children for effective living in society, or serving to interest children in school subjects. Such considerations find merit in controversial issues just because they may lead on to other activities considered worthwhile. But since we do not sensibly ask what is the *point* of education, it seems that educational activities are concerned with those learning experiences which are valued for their own sake. Hence an *educational* defence would need to point to something intrinsically worthwhile in controversial issues.

Stenhouse remarks that the decision to include controversial issues implies a value judgment.[8] Now clearly if one is drawing up an *educational* curriculum, it follows that the subjects included reflect the planner's views of what is intrinsically valuable. It needs to be remembered, however, that the very description of an issue as *controversial* is not value free for as the first and third conditions bring out, the issue is one which, for various reasons, *matters* to some people. Still, this is not enough for it does not follow that the issue is worthwhile in itself. Indeed this phrase rings somewhat strange, for we often seek to avoid controversy and regard it as undesirable.

This latter is, however, misleading for it blurs the distinction between the existence of controversy and the study of existing controversies. The latter may be intrinsically valuable even though the former is not. An analytic connection of the following kind can be made between the concept of education and the study of controversial issues. In many subjects, one can proceed a good way without getting into controversial matters.[9] As one approaches the frontiers of the discipline, however, it becomes logically impossible to avoid such issues if one is to do anything that would warrant the description of continuing to work in the discipline. Notice that I am not making the claim that it is logically necessary that controversy exist at the frontiers of a discipline, for it is logically possible for new theories to replace old without dispute. It is an empirical fact, however, that this does not happen; and given the existence of such controversy one would have a distorted view of the discipline if one were led to believe that it did not exist.

This may seem to be an argument based on *extrinsic* considerations, i.e., we study X (controversial issue) *in order* to pursue Y (e.g., history) which is intrinsically worthwhile.

Controversial Issues and the Teacher / 115

This, however, is a misdescription for X and Y are not properly separable. The study of X is a logically necessary part of the study of Y. For example, if it is considered educationally worthwhile to study the history of the English Civil War, one must also study the matters which are in dispute. Understanding the events involves coming to grasp where the lines of dispute are drawn. Hence, in any discipline or area of study where controversy exists, it is *prima facie* objectionable from an educational point of view to exclude such issues.

A fortiori, controversial value issues can only be eliminated at the risk of creating a distorted view of value questions and a distorted account of the issues. It is always possible to argue, however, that value issues in general (or any other traditional school subject) should not be included at all, in this way eliminating the need for consideration of controversies in those areas. At this point one could, of course, enter into a substantive debate concerning the worthwhileness of certain subjects, but I am persuaded that the following *formal* counter will suffice. The suggestion that certain subjects such as values, not be included at all, itself reflects a value judgment and one which is keenly disputed. A decision to exclude such an issue is not calculated to develop an understanding of the issue and distortion may result. This argument cannot be reversed to claim that inclusion of value issues begs the case against the exclusionists, for the views of the latter *can* (and, for one who employs the foregoing argument, logically *must*) be one of the controversial value issues openly discussed.[10]

I have, at best, sketched an *educational* consideration which creates a *prima facie* case for the inclusion of controversial issues, but nothing I have said entails a practical recommendation for including any specific issue at a specific time. And this is as it should be, for such practical recommendations are dependent too upon further evidence which philosophy *cannot* provide. For this reason, educational decision-making is an interdisciplinary affair. The *prima facie* case can, however, only be defeated by educationally relevant considerations, such as for example, psychological evidence that a certain group could not understand the issue, or sociological evidence that the presentation of the issue in any form would be likely to lead to a distorted grasp.

The arguments in this section depend in large measure upon an understanding of the concept of education, but the earlier analysis is relevant in that it brought out the points that controversial issues raise matters of serious concern and that progress towards resolution involves rational argument. They exist, moreover, *within* areas of human thought such that an understanding of that area involves an understanding of the controversy. *Rational* inquiry aimed at an *understanding* of *serious* issues picks out criteria which are quite central to our concept of becoming educated.

3. The Treatment of Controversial Issues

I shall imagine a situation in which the *prima facie* case has not been overthrown, and in which other educationally relevant considerations have led to the inclusion of a controversial issue in the classroom. How then is such an issue to be dealt with? It is, I believe, significant that among writers on social studies education there has been a marked preference for a term such as "handling" which suggests that the teacher needs to be wary, cautious and discreet. My remarks will, in effect, assess the appropriateness of the instinctive choice of a term with such connotations.

It was argued earlier that in the area of empirical disputes, the adjective "controversial" implies that the various positions in the dispute are taken seriously, and that at the moment the issue is not resolved. When the issue is settled, a correct answer will constitute a contribution to our knowledge. It is not part of the role of a teacher *qua teacher* to make a contribution to knowledge, as distinct from bringing others to knowledge, and bringing others to the point where they can make a contribution to knowledge.[11] It is true that teachers often do make contributions to a field of inquiry, but it is a point about the *concept* of teaching which is being made. But perhaps it will be suggested that at times a teacher is entitled, or has responsibility, to go beyond the confines of that role. And plausible examples can be found: at times a teacher has to be a counsellor. The difficulty of this argument in the context of teaching in the area of controversial empirical issues hinges on the fact that the teacher could only rarely be in a position to advance the public dispute. On such rare occasions, if he is able to advance the issue towards resolution, it follows that the issue ceases to be a controversial one. The obligation on the teacher to present the issue fairly, (and it is an analytic truth in such cases that each side has some merit) is derived from the concept of education which involves the pursuit of truth. An unsupported opinion from the teacher favoring one side does not contribute to this feature intrinsic to the idea of education. It might be thought that a case for teacher neutrality could be based on this point.[12] But the teacher who takes a stand on one side of a controversial issue may nevertheless do justice to other points of view, and present his own position as subject to revision. At times, of course, the appropriate stance for the teacher to adopt will be a neutral one.

Arguments in favor of neutrality in the area of controversial value issues are wide-spread,[13] but it seems logically impossible to provide a *general* argument in favor of neutrality in education for the following reason. As argued earlier, the concept of education implies that something worthwhile is being done. In being committed to education, a person is thereby committed to certain pursuits which he regards as valuable. Suppose that the nature of the controversial issue is such that the dispute concerns the *value* of such activities. For example, it is denied that students should be encouraged to think critically about current legislation. Adopting a neutral stand here amounts to giving up one's commitment. If it is argued by some that students should be indoctrinated, it is a conceptual truth that a teacher can only remain neutral on this at the cost of abandoning a commitment to education.

It might be argued, however, that it is one thing for a teacher to *have* a view on such an issue, and another to be entitled to *present* this view in class. But while this is a genuine distinction, it fails to operate in this case because if he continues to educate he is *ipso facto* taking a stand against indoctrination. Even to attempt to assess the arguments of the pro-indoctrination group is to fail to support them and hence to take a stand.

One reason which operates in specific cases in favor of neutrality is the same commitment to education, for in certain cases the arguments presented by the teacher for a particular view will only serve to indoctrinate the students.

118 / Controversies in Teaching

(Stenhouse claims, unrealistically I believe, that this is an inevitable outcome in *all* cases in public school.[14]) Indoctrination, however, is not the same form of miseducation which occurs when a teacher, without warrant, takes a stand on a controversial empirical dispute.

If, however, the situation is such that it is reasonable to judge that indoctrination will not result, then there appear to be cases in which the teacher is not obliged to remain neutral. Certain controversial value issues include positions against which good arguments can be developed. Other positions rest on claims for which there just is not any available evidence.[15] The teacher is not logically committed to showing that and how the arguments have reached stalemate, because such a state of affairs is not implied necessarily by the description "controversial" in such areas. And even in controversial empirical disputes where no resolution has been achieved, there is no reason in principle why a teacher cannot make it clear which side he finds most persuasive and why.

The word "handling" then is appropriate for in the case of empirical disputes the teacher must take care to avoid suggesting that we are closer to the truth than we are, and in the area of value disputes he must avoid the very real danger of indoctrination.

4. A Concluding Comment on Methodology

Methodological questions raise practical issues about which philosophy does not speak. But certain conceptual points are in order in connection with particular methods. Stenhouse correctly suggests the idea of principles of procedures being logically deducible from one's aims.[16] He wobbles at this point, however, by giving examples of procedures (e.g., committee procedure) which we know on *empirical* rather than *logical* grounds are useful in terms of the aim in question.

The method he favors, however, namely discussion, can be linked in a conceptual way with the aims of educational activities, but here I can only sketch such links. The connections seem to me to be twofold. First, if a person seriously enters into a discussion of an issue, his own views are in principle open to revision. Hence his views are being held in an openminded, non-dogmatic manner, which captures part of the notion of an educated outlook.[17] Secondly, partaking in a discussion involves a commitment to rational procedures, hence the idea of coercing the outcome can have no place. Education, too, conceptually involves a commitment to rational procedures. Having made such conceptual claims, however, all sorts of empirical questions remain, about when discussions are to be opened, and how precisely they are to be conducted and so on. We might even find that there were good grounds for *not* following such a procedure in certain circumstances.

Notes for Chapter Eleven: page 138

Chapter 12

The Roles of Teacher and Critic

1. Teaching and Criticism

I want to call attention to certain important differences between the activity of being a teacher and that of being a critic. We can begin by considering some conceptual points concerning the nature of teaching. It is of fundamental importance, I believe, that teaching as an activity cannot be categorized or defined without a reference to the concept of learning, for the meaning of the former is tied up with the latter in as much as teaching is an activity the aim of which is to produce learning (whatever that may be) in someone. I take it to be an intentional activity, meaning by that, that one cannot teach unintentionally, though I cannot argue for this here.[1] Furthermore, it is a polymorphous concept—that is to say, there are many different things one or another of which can in certain circumstances count as teaching, yet none of which in other circumstances necessarily counts as teaching. Though the activity can take many forms, the common feature is to be found in the aim of producing learning.

Thus, *qua teacher*, a person is not seeking to make a contribution to a body of knowledge, nor to add to the particular discipline he has mastered. Rather, he is attempting to bring others to share in the knowledge of the discipline which he has acquired himself. Of course a teacher may also make contributions to knowledge, but this is not his function as a teacher. Furthermore, a teacher may well hope to inspire his students to carry on and make a contribution themselves: and if they do, they may be able to do so because they had a good teacher. This does not affect the general point I am making. On the other hand *qua critic*, a person is making a contribution to the world of learning. A person who merely explains to another the criticisms of a particular writer is not fully engaging in the activity of criticism. We cannot simply adopt the views of others and be said to be "critical," though this is *not* to say that we cannot learn from the work of others. One qualification should be added to this criterion of "making a contribution." It is possible, though unlikely, that a critic could produce independently the same criticism as a previous writer, in ignorance of the earlier work. In such a case the later writer would not have literally "made a contribution," since his work had been anticipated—the contribution had already been made. All the same, it is vital here that the later writer did not know the earlier work, and he *saw himself* as making a contribution. This qualification will also cover the case of the work of a critic which proves unsuccessful, leads nowhere. Even though he fails to make a contribution, yet he has been engaging in criticism, for he intended to come up with judgments and assessments which would be valuable.

I do not want to suggest that when the ordinary theatregoer reflects on a play he has seen, he is not indulging in criticism unless he comes up with some comments of earth-shattering significance. This would rule out criticism as a possible activity for most of us. Usually, we simply classify the play under a generalization which we have found useful, or we evaluate the review of the play in the local paper. But I do suggest that criticism could not *all* be like this without eliminating a vital feature of the notion. Criticism is dead when it becomes stereotyped. This is another way of expressing the requirement which I call "making a contribution."

The fact that the teacher is necessarily trying to get someone to learn while the critic is primarily seeking to contribute to our ideas and thoughts about the arts makes a significant difference to the way in which they can set about their work. The teacher needs to gauge the state of mind of those whom he is teaching; otherwise his efforts will be in vain, and it is a necessary condition of a serious attempt to do something that one take care to prevent the aim being thwarted. Failure to take care would indicate a lack of seriousness, and if one were utterly careless it would be correct to say that he was not trying at all. Now all sorts of things can prevent a class from learning; for example, they may not be ready for the particular lesson. A teacher who wants to teach such a lesson must logically prepare the ground in the appropriate way: for if he does not, knowing the class is not ready, he cannot be said, in any serious way, to be teaching. For how can he be trying to get them to learn when he knows they will not? Now the critic, by contrast, is under no such obligation. He may, of course, have a burning desire to re-educate the tastes of the country, in which case he will attempt to prepare the ground. But a critic can continue his work although the world at large is not ready for his views, for this is true of any contributor to a body of knowledge. In this respect Roger Fry, who discussed the merits of Post-Impressionistic art long before people were ready for such views, was in the same situation as Galileo. Fry's activity *qua critic* was not jeopardized by the fact that his views were unpopular and hotly disputed. Of course teachers too may take a long time to get through to their students, but the important difference does not concern the length of time. Rather, it is not necessarily part of the function of the critic to get the public to understand or believe his views. Others can do this for him.

2. *The Teacher as Critic*

I have spoken of a critic as contributing to a body of knowledge; a commitment on my part to a particular epistemological classification of aesthetic judgments should not be read into this. My general point will hold even if aesthetic judgments are classified as no more than interesting and novel ways of considering art objects. For I do want to acknowledge the evaluative aspects to the work of the critic. An explicit appraisal of the work of art is aimed at, although it doesn't follow that the critic is concerned to draw up a list of the best paintings in order of merit: we don't have to see paintings competing with each other in this sort of way even if we do want to make general comparisons between the fine and the shoddy. Nevertheless, the critic will want to use terms of evaluation and will regard painting X as good for a variety of reasons. Now it is a fact that our teachers in schools and universities do regard pupil X as good for a variety of reasons. But is this only a contingent fact, or is it a necessary aspect of teaching, as it is a necessary aspect of criticism? Much of the recent discussion of the question of examinations and evaluation in education has been heavily emotion-laden, and unduly influenced by what William James called "the philosophy of tenderness in education." ("Talks to Teachers.") One point clearly follows from my earlier discussion of a "serious attempt" to do something; namely, that a teacher must logically take care to see if he's getting across—he must somehow determine if the students are learning. But here a difference emerges, for what *may* result is not an evaluation of the *student* (in comparison to evaluation of the work of art), but rather an evaluation of the *teaching performance.* It is the teaching performance which may have to be assessed even if many students in the group have learned as a result of the performance. For it certainly doesn't necessarily follow that those who have failed to learn are in some way at fault: this is clear from our classification of teaching as a polymorphous concept. What counts as teaching in one set of circumstances (with one type of student) won't necessarily count as teaching in another set of circumstances (that is, with a different type of student). Now even if I am correct that teaching necessarily involves this kind of assessment, it doesn't follow of course that this assessment is part of the role of the teacher; this is clear because in certain circumstances the assessment could be done by others, and secondly the teaching is completed before assessment is possible, if we are assessing what has been learned.

We might examine how the two roles relate to the concept of authority. Teachers are often placed in authority while critics are not, but there is nothing necessary about this. Socrates was not placed in a position of authority, and some critics are appointed to chairs in universities. More interestingly, a teacher can often claim to be an authority on a subject which he has mastered. But this is not necessarily the case, and this not simply because the teacher may not be well up in his subject. Rather, my point is that the notion of teaching is at home when we don't have a subject in the sense of a body of knowledge at all. We can teach people a sense of responsibility; but in what sense could anyone be an authority on this matter? The point can be seen by realizing that we can teach students to be critical, but this involves much more than the passing on of a body of rules and collection of knowledge which the teacher has mastered. Now the question at hand is, can the critic ever claim to be *an* authority? I think the answer here is surely "Yes," and we can cite people like Roger Fry, T. S. Eliot, and F. R. Leavis. But we do not mean by this that they, like the teacher of an academic subject, have mastered some particular body of knowledge, although they have indeed a great knowledge of the work of the artists which they have studied. Nor do we mean they have produced theories and judgments which are objectively true in some unproblematic sense. As Margaret MacDonald,[2] following Wordsworth, has commented, we are not argued into a favorable verdict on works of art, for all that the critic employs reasons rather than personal reactions. We can, by contrast, be argued into accepting a conclusion in science, and the teacher attempts to do so. These remarks in no way imply subjectivism in aesthetics, but only recognize that aesthetic judgments are not arrived at by deductive or inductive procedures.

At this point I must anticipate an objection to my account of the role of a teacher. I have been indicating what a teacher can do, and it has emerged that he can instruct, influence, argue, and so on. And it may be asked if this is what the role of a teacher *ought* to be: we cannot avoid the normative question because roles can be assigned to people and different roles may be compatible with the one concept. The objection is really whether or not the teacher should play the sort of positive role I have been suggesting. Historically a counter to this position has been developed by such writers as Comenius, Rousseau, and Froebel. The kind of language employed by such writers, for example, the famous "plant" metaphor, indicates the kind of role the teacher should play. If the question at hand were the debate between child-centered and authoritative approaches to education (not that these are clear-cut distinctions, mutually exclusive, or exhaustive alternatives) my sympathies would be with Professor Bantock when he accuses the child-centered theorists of inconsistency[3] in the development of their views. Nevertheless, we can agree that these theorists have important suggestions to make concerning the manner in which the teacher should set about his task. Certainly the view I have sketched is compatible with the role of a teacher in a child-centered situation. There is necessarily a variety of ways in which one can set about producing learning. An essential feature would be lost, for example, if we took Rousseau literally when he says that the great thing is to do nothing. This is an exaggeration for all that the good teacher will know when to say nothing and to stand back. The teacher does not always have to be *giving* criticism.

3. *The Critic as Teacher*

In so far as criticism offers the verdicts of people who have achieved the status of "authorities," it can put us on to a good work in the same way as a teacher can. At this level, however, the didactic element is minimal, and this is an area where Scheffler's distinction between teaching and *telling* would be applicable. In the classroom situation what can make "telling" into "teaching" is the aspect we noted earlier of the *appropriate moment*, that is, the teacher judges that now is the time to tell the pupil of a particular author's works. Occasionally the critic is able to exercise his judgment in this sort of way, for example, by publishing an article in a newspaper at the right moment. Thus, the "verdict" aspect of criticism can count as teaching sometimes, but our main interest is not with the verdict but with the reasons given in support of it. For it is these which can help us to understand and appreciate the work of art.

But as we noticed earlier, although the critic gives us reasons, we are not being argued into an evaluation. For what we call an aesthetic "argument" does not fall into either the deductive or the inductive mode of reasoning. The critic's reasons may enable us to *see* the work of art in the way in which he thinks it should be seen. Of course part of the critic's task in analyzing a complex work of art will be to call our attention to features we have failed to notice. But apart from this there is also the task of redirecting our attention to things we have noticed but failed to recognize for what they are. On these occasions we can have that experience which Wittgenstein called "noticing an aspect."[4] His example here is that of looking at a face and suddenly noticing its resemblance to another. The face has not changed yet we see it differently. T. S. Eliot was making the same point when he expressed gratitude to the critic who "can make me look at something I have never looked at before, or looked at only with eyes clouded with prejudice."[5] Eliot goes on, however, to say that after this the critic should leave him alone with the work, for in the last analysis the spectator, listener, reader, has to appreciate the work *himself*. Jerome Stolnitz has some good things to say about the ways in which criticism actually hinders a person's appreciation even if the criticism is sound.[6] He is concerned with the "educative function" of criticism; so perhaps it is natural that he should stress the didactic aspects of criticism. He praises intrinsic criticism for guiding perception to what is hidden beneath the surface (this could be an example of "noticing an aspect"). But he points out that a student may not be able to absorb *all the meanings* which he has learned into his aesthetic perception: and thus these many meanings fail to intensify the aesthetic experience. However, it would seem that Stolnitz passes from saying what the educative function of criticism can be, to saying what it must be. He refers to such a situation as the one of the student who fails to absorb all the meanings as an example of "the errors of criticism." The critic is decried for being more interested in scholarship than the enjoyment of art. But this is an unfair set of alternatives and misdescribes the situation. The critic *is* concerned with the enjoyment of art: his criticism only counts as criticism if it can lead to a heightened appreciation of art. But there is no reason why the critic *must* be concerned to spread such enjoyment around. Secondly, the failure may be on the part of the student. If he isn't capable of absorbing the criticism, this is no reflection on the criticism. Perhaps he can be brought to appreciate it, and perhaps even now others do appreciate it. I want to agree, then, that criticism has didactic aspects and that the most important of these is to bring us to see something in a new way. But a work of criticism is not bad if we fail to see something in this way, for the failure may lie in ourselves. It may take a lesser person to *get* me to see what Leavis or Eliot has *enabled* us to see. Such a person is a lesser critic, but perhaps a better teacher (at one level at least). Stolnitz appears to support his emphasis on the didactic aspect of criticism by remarking that interpretation and value-judgments must always be tested in aesthetic experience. "They do not prove themselves. They are proved when the interpretation can be used fruitfully within aesthetic awareness." I would agree that aesthetic judgments are tested in aesthetic awareness but I don't see that this brings out the didactic nature of criticism; for the critic can "test" his views in his own aesthetic awareness. He doesn't have to consider "the goodness that people actually feel in their encounter with the work."

As our interest here is in the didactic aspects of criticism we might notice that some writers (Margaret MacDonald, for one)[7] have found it puzzling that a critic *can* make us "notice an aspect": "But it is not quite clear what information is being given by the critic and how." Miss MacDonald is not here raising a psychological question, nor a question concerning the technique of the critic. She finds something logically puzzling in the way that a critic can bring us to *see* what we had not seen. For it is quite true, as Miss MacDonald observes, that discussion does not improve eyesight and hearing. It isn't simply that the critic can give new information which will help our *understanding*. Let us consider John Wisdom's famous example in which a man fails to recognize the object in front of him as a snake until someone shouts "Snake!" Now, it seems to me that this is not so much a case in which discussion aids our understanding, but more nearly a case where discussion helps us to see. The appropriate comment is surely not "Now I understand," but "Now I see." The *word* "snake" helped us here. Professor Sibley[8] provides a very valuable list of the sorts of things which critics say. Sometimes the critic will simply point out things which we have not noticed (this is different from "noticing an aspect"); for example, "Did you notice the small figure in the foreground?" Sometimes however, he will help us in much the same way as the man who shouts "snake!" Sibley refers to this as mentioning the very qualities we want people to see: for example, "Notice how nervous and delicate the drawing is." Now, of course, this is not an exact counterpart of Wisdom's example, for "nervousness" is an interpretation in a way that "snake" is not (though I realize that this is more a matter of degree than quality for "snake" is also interpretive). But like "snake", "nervous" and "delicate" require no *argument*: the words are themselves sufficient, or at least they can be so. The basic point here is of course that what we *see* is determined by our conceptual framework. We may have these concepts, as the man obviously had the concept of "snake", yet it may take someone else to convince us that here is an occasion which requires the concept. And the critic often has this function.

When we consider the critic's use of language which employs analogy and metaphor, we come closer to the notion of "information which aids our understanding." How is it that we learn when the critic tells us that, for example, a particular artist's paintings are "fires"? If this is the general problem, then I am in sympathy with Sibley's view that there is in fact no real puzzle here. In the first place, he points out that between literal language and full-blown metaphorical language, as in "His paintings are fires," there are intermediate stages. Words like "nervous" which have a literal use are employed by analogy. As Sibley points out, it is a feature of human intelligence that we are able to spot similarities. With children we can begin by employing the simpler quasi-metaphorical concepts—a simple piece of music is said to be "running." There is a *natural* association here, for children are likely to run (literally) with the music if they are allowed to do so. Sibley's method then is the time-honored one in philosophy of pointing out that something which strikes us as puzzling is only one step away from something else which isn't puzzling at all.

Notes for Chapter Twelve: pages 138-139

Notes

Notes for Introduction
1. For a recent example, see Carl Knape and Paul T. Rosewell, "The Philosophically Discerning Classroom Teacher," in *Educational Studies*, II, 1, 1980, pp. 37-47. See also my comments in "Philosophical Discernment and Teaching: a Response to Knape and Rosewell," in *Educational Studies*, 12, 3, 1981, pp. 281-286.
2. For this sort of view, see John Colbeck, "Criticizing Critical Philosophy of Education," in *Journal of Further and Higher Education*, 4, 2, 1980, pp. 60-72. I have dealt with these and related criticisms in my paper "The Attack on Open-mindedness," *Oxford Review of Education*, 7, 2, 1981.
3. See David Braybrooke, "How Philosophy Helps in Social Studies," *Journal of Education* (Nova Scotia), 7, 2, March 1981, pp. 16-19.
4. It is now a commonplace, for example, to hold that there are several *senses* of leadership. But is there any reason to believe that this is so?
5. H. L. A. Hart, *The Concept of Law*, London: Oxford University Press, 1961, p. 7.
6. See also my paper "Philosophy and Practical Advice," in *Journal of Education* (Nova Scotia), 7, 2, March 1981, pp. 3-5.
7. See also Bertrand Russell, *The Problems of Philosophy*, London: Oxford University Press, 1959, pp. 89-94.
8. See also my paper "Education and Citizenship," in *Contact*, 48, February, 1981.

Notes for Chapter One
1. *New Dimensions in Education*, Toronto (June, 1970).
2. Michael Hutchinson and Christopher Young, *Educating the Intelligent*, Harmondsworth: Penguin Books, 1966, p. 105.
3. For a discussion of this point see John Hanson, "Learning by Experience," in B. Othanel Smith and Robert H. Ennis (eds.), *Language and Concepts in Education*, Chicago: Rand McNally & Company, 1961.
4. Professor R. S. Peters has argued for this conceptual link in his *Ethics and Education*, London: George Allen and Unwin, 1966.

Notes for Chapter Two
1. David Hume, *An Inquiry Concerning the Principles of Morals*, Section III, Part I.
2. See further Chapter Seven.

3. John Passmore, "On Teaching to be Critical," in R. S. Peters (ed.), *The Concept of Education*, London: Routledge and Kegan Paul, 1967.
4. For other comments on the concept of relevance, see Kingsley Price, "On Educational Relevance and Irrelevance," in James F. Doyle (ed.), *Educational Judgments*, London: Routledge and Kegan Paul, 1973; also Israel Scheffler, "Reflections on Educational Relevance," in R. S. Peters (ed.), *The Philosophy of Education*, London: Oxford University Press, 1973.

Notes for Chapter Three
1. For example, one encounters articles in educational theory with titles such as, "Continuing Change is Needed." For this paper by Allan Glatthorn see Dwight W. Allen and Jeffrey C. Hecht (eds.), *Controversies in Education*, Philadelphia: W. B. Saunders, 1974, pp. 103-9.
2. Notably Richard Pratte, "Innovation in Education," *Philosophy of Education 1974: Proceedings of the Thirtieth Annual Meeting of the Philosophy of Education Society*, Michael J. Parsons (ed.), Edwardsville, Ill.: Philosophy of Education Society, 1974, pp. 363-74.
3. *Ibid.*, p. 363.
4. *Ibid.* The painting is not an *accident*, and thus this case is not the same as Pratte's example of the French chef who goofs.
5. For further discussion of the concept of judgment, see my paper, "The Teaching of Judgment," *British Journal of Educational Studies*, XIX, 3, 1971, pp. 243-49.
6. An instance, if you like, of innovation in the conceptual realm.
7. Pratte, "Innovation in Education," p. 365.
8. See *The Philosophy of Education*, R. S. Peters (ed.) London: Oxford University Press, 1973, pp. 40-41. For another example see William Frankena, "The Principles of Morality," in *Skepticism and Moral Principles*, C. Carter (ed.), Evanston, Ill.: New University Press, 1973.
9. Sometimes the actual employment of scare-quotes is not needed. Thus, Sidney Hook can write: "But there are very few careers that can be adequately prepared for by bull-sessions and innovative courses uncontrolled by competent faculty supervision." See *The Philosophy of the Curriculum*, Sidney Hook, Paul Kurtz and Milo Todorovich (eds.), Buffalo: Prometheus Books, 1975, p. xii. But the reader is left in no doubt as to Hook's assessment of what are called "innovative" courses.
10. Pratte, "Innovation in Education," p. 366.
11. Many practices which we take to be very modern, e.g., work outside a classroom, discovery learning, discussion methods, are clearly exemplified in the teaching of Socrates.
12. Herbert I. VonHaden and Jean Marie King, *Educational Innovator's Guide*, Worthington, Ohio: Charles A. Jones, 1974, p. v.

13. See Glatthorn, "Continuing Change," in *Controversies*, p. 103. It is interesting to note, however, that at one point he speaks of "so-called innovations."
14. Even Denisovich, who wanted to get sick, added "not fatally or anything that needed an operation." See Alexander Solzhenitsyn, *One Day in the Life of Ivan Denisovich*, New York: Bantam Books, 1973, p. 23.
15. Sidney Hook, "Illich's DeSchooled Utopia," *Radical School Reform*, Cornelius J. Troost (ed.), Boston: Little Brown, 1973.
16. "Significant" is ambiguous sometimes meaning "of value", e.g., a significant contribution. Here I am using it to mean "sufficiently different" as explained in Section I.
17. Glatthorn, "Continuing Change," in *Controversies*, p. 103. "Supposedly" — another example of the external descriptive comment.
18. Or conversely, detect a continuity where change had been alleged. I am reminded here of the reported phenomenon of desks, bookcases, and other items of furniture serving to substitute for walls in open-plan schools.
19. John Holt, *Escape from Childhood*, New York: Ballantine Books, 1974, p. 47. See the following chapter for a detailed critique of Holt's views.
20. "Registry of Innovative Practices Created," *Canadian Education Newsletter*, (March 1975), p. 1.
21. See footnotes 12 and 20.
22. See VonHaden and King, *Educational Innovator's Guide*, Preface and Acknowledgements.
23. Alan White, "Needs and Wants," *Proceedings of the Philosophy of Education Society of Great Britain*, 8, 2, 1974, p. 177.

Notes for Chapter Four
1. See John Kemp, "The Work of Art and the Artist's Intention," *British Journal of Aesthetics*, 4, 2, 1964, pp. 146-54.
2. Jerry Hirsch, "Jensenism: The Bankruptcy of 'Science' without Scholarship," *Educational Theory*, 25, 1, 1975, pp. 3-27. Hirsch accuses Hernstein of adopting the credentialist philosophy (p. 7, fn. 22), yet later berates scholars for considering views "proposed by no matter whom, published no matter where" (p. 27). I call attention to this in case it should be overlooked, occurring as it does in the same paragraph as Hirsch manages to suggest that the financial plight of university libraries should be added to the list of charges against Jensen! Reading this, one is bound to wonder if Scriven was not overly generous in regarding the majority of work on the "Jensen affair" as totally incompetent by the standards of a Psychology 1 course. See "The Values of the Academy," *Review of Educational Research*, 40, 4, 1970, pp. 541-49.
3. The most penetrating analysis is Alan White, "Needs and Wants," *Proceedings of the Philosophy of Education Society of Great Britain*, 8, 2, 1974, pp. 159-80.

4. The criticism here is that Holt is inconsistent. I say nothing as such on the substantive moral question involved which seems to me to be very complex. Is it, for example, entirely clear that wearing a seat belt is a purely self-regarding action (to use Mill's language)?
5. I borrow this phrase from John Rawls, *A Theory of Justice*, Cambridge, Mass.: Belknap Press, 1971, p. 101.
6. See my paper "The Disappearing Teacher" in Michael J. B. Jackson (ed.), *Schools, Freedom and Authority*, St. Johns: Memorial University, 1975, pp. 3-12.
7. A small point, perhaps, but Holt fails to indicate that it is not always a misfortune. This is simply one more example of Holt's failure to provide the requisite qualifications to his claims.
8. A. J. Ayer, *The Problem of Knowledge*, Harmondsworth: Penguin Books, 1956, p. 30.

Notes for Chapter Five
1. Thus, no difficulties are encountered when we find an article entitled "Film Appreciation as Aesthetic Education," Ralph A. Smith, *Educational Forum*, 30, 4, 1966, pp. 483-89, even though Smith nowhere gives an analysis of the concept. It is significant, however, that his concern in the paper is to get clearer about the peculiar nature of film, and this does not demand a precise account of what is meant by appreciation.
2. *Cf.* an 1864 usage which speaks of a man being very severe in his appreciation.
3. Here I am indebted to Alan White's paper, "Meaning and Implication," *Analysis*, 32, 1971, pp. 26-30.
4. I can, however, admire the achievements of Einstein without understanding them. I understand that they were remarkable achievements and am entitled to believe on other grounds that they were significant.
5. H. Osborne, *The Art of Appreciation*, New York: Oxford University Press, 1970, p. 16.
6. See B. Othanel Smith, "The Logic of Teaching in the Arts," reprinted in Ralph A. Smith, (ed.), *Aesthetics and Criticism in Art Education*, Chicago: Rand McNally, 1966, pp. 46-55.
7. See Dick Field, *Change in Art Education*, London: Routledge and Kegan Paul, 1970, p. 110.
8. Thomas Munro, *Evolution in the Arts*, Cleveland: Cleveland Museum of Art, 1963, p. 400.
9. Smith, "The Logic of Teaching in the Arts," pp. 50-51.
10. *Cf.* Alan White's argument against the identification of "feeling sure" and "knowing" in "On Claiming to Know," reprinted in A. Phillips Griffiths, (ed.), *Knowledge and Belief*, London: Oxford University Press, 1967, pp. 100-111.
11. See Chapter One for the view that understanding a subject does not involve being committed to its pursuit.

12. See a discussion of this point in Elliot W. Eisner and David W. Ecker, "Some Historical Developments in Art Education," reprinted in George Pappas, (ed.), *Concepts in Art and Education*, London: MacMillan, 1970, p. 17.

Notes for Chapter Six
1. Ruth Landes, "Culture and Education," George F. Kneller, (ed.), in *Foundations of Education*, New York, John Wiley and Sons, Inc., 1963, pp. 320-352.
2. *Ibid.*, p. 324.
3. I have discussed certain aspects of this attitude in my paper, "The MacKay Report on Religious Education: A Critical Commentary," *Teacher Education*, Spring 1971, pp. 16-23. The reader is also referred to R. S. Downie and Elizabeth Telfer, *Respect for Persons*, London: George Allen and Unwin, 1969.
4. On the logic of teaching in this area, the reader should consult "On Teaching to be Critical," J. A. Passmore, in R. S. Peters, (ed.), *The Concept of Education*, London, Routledge and Kegan Paul, 1967, pp. 192-211; and my paper, "The Teaching of Judgment," *British Journal of Educational Studies*, XIX, 3, 1971, pp. 243-249.
5. For a thorough discussion of these ideas, see my *Open-mindedness and Education*, Montreal: McGill-Queen's University Press, 1979.

Notes for Chapter Seven
1. The composition of the Study Committee of a recent Canadian inquiry into emotional and learning disorders clearly reflects this. See *One Million Children: The Celdic Report*, Canada, 1970, p. 29. There is a dearth of analytical work on the concept of culture. *Cf.* the comments of R. G. Woods and Robin Barrow in *An Introduction to Philosophy of Education*, London: Methuen, 1975, p. 193.
2. See the discussion in Chapter Six.
3. Kenneth R. Johnson, *Teaching the Culturally Disadvantaged*, California: Palo Alto, 1970, p. 2. Examples are readily multiplied. Mary Ashworth in "Results and Issues from a National Survey of ESL Programmes," in Aaron Wolfgang (ed.), *Education of Immigrant Students: Issues and Answers*, Toronto: Ontario Institute for Studies in Education, 1975, pp. 84-94 asserts, without argument, with respect to the immigrant student that "his differences need to be seen simply as that — differences, not handicaps or afflictions or some form of inferior behavior." See my review of this book in *The History and Social Science Teacher*, 12, 1, 1976, p. 60.
4. David Hume, *An Enquiry Concerning the Principles of Morals*, Section 1.
5. Johnson, *op. cit.*, p. 9.

6. This position is most eloquently expressed and ably defended in Israel Scheffer, "Reflections on Educational Relevance," *Journal of Philosophy*, 66, 1969, pp. 764-73.
7. John Rawls, *A Theory of Justice*, Cambridge, Mass.: Belknap Press, 1971, p. 101.

Notes for Chapter Eight
1. "Apology," in Raphael Demos, (ed.), *Plato Selections*, New York: Charles Scribner's Sons, 1955, p. 4.
2. Demos, *op. cit.*, particularly pp. 51-59. See also *Meno* 90D.
3. Rousseau, *Considerations Concerning the Government of Poland and its Projected Reform*. See Kingsley Price, *Education and Philosophical Thought*, Boston: Allyn & Bacon, Inc., 1962, p. 348.
4. John Holt, *Freedom and Beyond*, New York: Dell Publishing Co., Inc., 1972, p. 225.
5. Herbert Kohl, *Reading, How To*, New York: E. P. Dutton & Co. Inc., 1973, pp. 3-9.
6. *Op. cit.*, p. 3.
7. *Op. cit.*, p. 5.
8. *Op. cit.*, p. 10.
9. *Op. cit.*, p. 4
10. Demos, *op. cit.*, p. 58.
11. *Op. cit.*, p. 63.
12. Kohl, *op. cit.*, p. 5.
13. See my paper, "The Concept of Reading: A Philosophical Analysis," in *Journal of Reading Behavior*, 5, 2, 1973, pp. 152-155.
14. Kohl, *op. cit.*, p. 3; *cf.* his comments on reading Freire.
15. To those who object that I have taken Kohl too literally, I make no apology. For apart from the internal evidence (for example, his discussion of the word "remediation") that he values the clear and precise use of language, there is absolutely no reason to believe that he is *not* speaking literally. In the absence of such reasons, it seems to me to be a serious discourtesy to a person to suggest that he did not intend what his words plainly mean.
16. *Cf.* my paper, "The Teaching of Judgment," in *British Journal of Educational Studies*, XIX, 3, 1971, pp. 243-249.
17. See Chapter Nine.
18. Donna H. Kerr and Jonas F. Soltis, "Locating Teacher Competency: An Action Description of Teaching," in *Educational Theory*, 24, 1, 1974, pp. 3-16.
19. I am not, of course, using the word "purpose" in the sense of "ulterior purposes" which Peter Winch rightly decries in his paper "The Universities and the State," *Universities Quarterly*, 12, 1, 1957, pp. 14-23.
20. The conceptual and normative issue does become relevant in the case where we are deciding whether to appoint X or Y, when X is

superior in terms of research pursuits. But such a dilemma does not show that attention to the candidates teaching ability is not at all relevant—quite the contrary.
21. See, for example, *A Choice of Futures*, Report of the Commission on Educational Planning, (Queen's Printer for the Province of Alberta, 1972), pp. 244-5. This document is often referred to as *The Worth Report*. They support initial training, without *formal* certification. But, of course, if initial training is taken seriously, there must be some form of public scrutiny. If the *justification* of training is to approach some standard of achievement, then it must be worth asking if this standard has been reached.

Notes for Chapter Nine
1. J. G. McMurray, "Theory and Practice," *Teacher Education*, 3, Spring 1970, p. 33.
2. See my paper "The Teaching of Judgment," *British Journal of Educational Studies*, XIX, 3, 1971, pp. 243-49.
3. See Chapter One.
4. B. O. Smith, *Teachers for the Real World*, AACTE, Washington, D.C., 1969, p. 93.
5. *Teacher Education: Perseverence or Professionalism*, Committee on Teacher Education, University of Prince Edward Island, pp. 5-15.
6. Ivan Illich, "The Alternative to Schooling," *Saturday Review*, June 19, 1971, pp. 44-60.
7. B. Paul Komisar, "Teaching: Act and Enterprise," in C. J. B. MacMillan and Thomas W. Nelson, (eds.), *Concepts of Teaching, Philosophical Essays*, Chicago: Rand McNally, 1968, pp. 63-68.
8. I. Scheffler, "Philosophical Models of Teaching" in Ronald T. Hyman (ed.), *Contemporary Thought on Teaching*, Englewood Cliffs: Prentice-Hall, 1971, pp. 173-83.

Notes for Chapter Ten
1. This remains true in 1983.
2. *Cf.* John Passmore, "On Teaching to be Critical," in R. S. Peters (ed.), *The Concept of Education*, London: Routledge and Kegan Paul, 1967, p. 210.
3. See Israel Scheffler, *Reason and Teaching*, Indianapolis: Bobbs-Merrill, 1973. Of particular relevance here is Chapter 3 'Philosophy and the Curriculum,' from which the significance of the distinction between the researcher and the teacher discussed earlier is derived.
4. *Program of Studies in the Schools of Nova Scotia*, Halifax: Department of Education, 1974, p. 7.
5. I refer to the work of the Institute for the Advancement of Philosophy for Children, at Montclair State College, New Jersey. See, in particular, Mathew Lipman, *Harry Stottlemeier's Discovery*, New Jersey: Montclair State College, 1971, and

Mathew Lipman and Ann Margaret Sharp, *Teaching Children Philosophical Thinking*. Mention should also be made of the journal, *Teaching Philosophy*, from the University of Cincinnatti.

Notes for Chapter Eleven
1. L. Stenhouse, "Controversial Value Issues in the Classroom," in *Values and the Curriculum*. A report of the Fourth International Curriculum Conference, edited by William G. Carr. Washington: National Education Association Publications, 1970, pp. 103-15.
2. *Op. cit.*, p. 103.
3. Graham Chedd, "The Need to Understand," An interview with Linus Pauling, *New Scientist and Science Journal*, June 24, 1971, pp. 753-55.
4. Stenhouse, *op. cit.*, p. 103.
5. *Op. cit.*, p. 104.
6. *Op. cit.*, p. 104. That he is wrong here can be seen from the fact that his claim would itself be controversial.
7. Has, for example, Erich von Daniken been sufficiently disturbing in *Chariots of the Gods?*
8. Stenhouse, *op. cit.*, p. 107.
9. Jerome Schaffer makes the point that in philosophy it is often a short trek to the frontier. See *Reality Knowledge and Value*, New York: Random House, 1971, p. vii.
10. See also my discussion of a related point in "The Attack on Openmindedness," *Oxford Review of Education*, 7, 2, 1981, pp. 119-129.
11. See Chapter Twelve.
12. The *possibility* of neutrality, sometimes questioned by philosophers, has been made out to my satisfaction in "The Possibility of Neutrality," Robert Ennis, *Educational Theory*, 19, 4, 1969, pp. 347-56.
13. See Stenhouse, *op. cit.*, p. 106.
14. *Op. cit.*, p. 106.
15. *Cf.* Kurt Baier's comments on the injunction against eating pork, in the discussion section of C. M. Beck, B. A. Crittenden, and E. V. Sullivan (eds.), *Moral Education: Interdisciplinary Approaches*, Toronto: University of Toronto Press, 1971, p. 295.
16. Stenhouse, *op. cit.*, p. 108.
17. These ideas are developed in my *Open-mindedness and Education*, Montreal: McGill-Queen's University Press, 1979.

Notes for Chapter Twelve
1. In contrast see the paper by F. A. Siegler in *The Discipline of Education*, J. Walton and J. L. Kuethe Madison (eds.), 1963, pp. 40-46.
2. "Some Distinctive Features of Arguments Used in Criticism of the Arts," reprinted in *Essays in Aesthetics and Language*, W. Elton (ed.), Oxford: Blackwell, 1954.

Notes / 139

3. "The Role of the Teacher," G. M. Bantock in *Education, Culture and the Emotions*, London: Faber, 1967, p. 137.
4. *Philosophical Investigations*, Oxford: Blackwell, 1963, p. 193.
5. "The Frontiers of Criticism," in *On Poetry and Poets*, London: Faber and Faber, 1957, p. 117.
6. See *Aesthetics and Philosophy of Art Criticism*, Boston: Houghton Mifflin, 1960, pp. 493-501.
7. *Op. cit.*, p. 120. She does not actually employ the phrase "notice an aspect."
8. See "Aesthetic Concepts," *Philosophical Review*, LXVIII, 1959, pp. 421-50.

Other titles of interest:

MAN AND NATURE
Papers of the Canadian Society for Eighteenth-Century Studies/Vol. 1.
Edited by R. L. Emerson, G. Girard and R. Runte
1982, cloth

GIVING TEACHING BACK TO TEACHERS
A Critical Introduction to Curriculum Theory
Robin Barrow
1984, paperback

INJUSTICE, INEQUALITY AND ETHICS
Robin Barrow
Reprinted 1983, paperback

THE PHILOSOPHY OF SCHOOLING
Robin Barrow
Reprinted 1983, paperback

Additional details from:
WHEATSHEAF BOOKS
16 Ship Street
Brighton, Sussex
England BN1 1AD

THE ALTHOUSE PRESS
Faculty of Education
The University of Western Ontario
London, Ontario
Canada N6G 1G7